Science of Mind Skills
by
Jane Claypool

Cornucopia Press
P.O. Box 230638
Encinitas, CA 92023

Copyright © 1997 by Jane Claypool.

All rights reserved. Except for brief quotations used in articles or reviews, no part of this publication may be reproduced or transmitted in any form by any means, electronic or mechanical, including photocopying, recording, or any information storage/retrieval system, without written permission.

ISBN 0-9643948-2-0

For my beloved daughter, Kate DuVivier.
You are love and light.

TABLE OF CONTENTS

Author's Introduction		1
One	Simple To Understand - A Challenge to Live By	7
Two	You Have Choices	13
Three	In The Name Of God	17
Four	Your Relationship To God	21
Five	A Spiritual Universe	25
Six	Spirit Is The Basis Of Life	29
Seven	Your Message Center	31
Eight	You Are The Director	35
Nine	You Are Attractive	39
Ten	Power Now	41
Eleven	You Are Responsible	45
Twelve	Prayer Treatment	49
Thirteen	Recognizing God	53
Fourteen	Unification or Identification	55
Fifteen	I Declare	59
Sixteen	Handling Objections	63
Seventeen	I Accept The Best	67
Eighteen	Let Go and Let God	69
Nineteen	Using Intuition	71
Twenty	It Is All One	75
Twenty-One	One God - Two Functions	79

Twenty-Two	Evil Disappears In The Light Of Truth	83
Twenty-Three	Choosing Positive Experiences	87
Twenty-Four	You Always Have A Choice	91
Twenty-Five	Positive Proof	95
Twenty-Six	Healthy Relationships	99
Twenty-Seven	You Are Not A Victim	103
Twenty-Eight	Begin With Self Love	107
Twenty-Nine	Abundant Life	111
Thirty	Money and Spirit	113
Thirty-One	Attracting Money	117
Thirty-Two	Money, Money, Money	121
Thirty-Three	Paying The Price	125
Thirty-Four	Rags To Riches	131
Thirty-Five	Right Work	135
Thirty-Six	My Work Is Completed	139
Thirty-Seven	I Demonstrate Success	141
Thirty-Eight	I Love My Body	145
Thirty-Nine	My Perfect Body	149
Forty	No Chronic Conditions	151
Forty-One	Highest and Best	155
Forty-Two	I Move Forward	157
Forty-Three	Be Happy Now	159
Forty-Four	No Hidden Blocks	161
Forty-Five	I Am Not Discouraged	164

Forty-Six	Fast Action	169
Forty-Seven	I Choose My Experience	173
Forty-Eight	Unlimited Energy	177
Forty-Nine	Expect The Best	181
Fifty	The Immanence Of God	185
Fifty-One	God And I Are One	189
Fifty-Two	A Final Word About Church Attendance	193

SCIENCE OF MIND SKILLS

AUTHOR'S INTRODUCTION

I came into Religious Science gradually, over a period of many years, and books were a large part of my learning experience so it is probably natural that I place such a special value on the power of metaphysical books. Others find classes and tapes the easiest way to assimilate these ideas but I was able to learn best from books, partly because I was so alienated from others that I found it easier to trust what I read than what I heard.

I liked going to church (at least when I was doing well) but what I heard in church didn't seem to have much to do with the life I was living. I was one of those silent churchgoers who came late and left early so she didn't have to hold hands. Books didn't ask you questions or try to put you on committees.

Between 1956 when I was introduced to Religious Science and 1989 when I was licensed as a minister, my reading melted into a soup pot of metaphysical, philosophical and psychological ideas. Eventually, I had to take spiritual nourishment in a way I could understand and accept for myself.

My acceptance of Science of Mind principles was really by process of distillation. I'd studied or experimented with yoga, Zen, Judaism, Tarot cards, psychic phenomenon, 12 step recovery programs, political activism, and psychological counseling.

While I learned a great deal from some of those activities and still continue to be active in 12 step programs and to meditate daily, I eventually discarded or distanced myself from everything else except Science of Mind. I stuck with Science of Mind because it is positive, powerful, and provable.

Though slow to learn, my conviction runs deep and when I became a minister, I established a personal goal of teaching Science of Mind ideas and skills to as many people as possible - through books as well as in my own church.

While I was studying for the ministry, my task was often to separate Science of Mind from layers of encrusted opinion, beliefs and supposition that were my own mental overlays. Somehow, I imagined my first books would have something to do with that theme.

I quickly discovered that there were other, more pressing needs. Our small church bookstore stocked a variety of books - any metaphysical based book whose central message was that the power lies within you - but we didn't have a really simple beginners' book. People kept asking for a book that would show them how to use the basic ideas of Science of Mind in their lives. They weren't as interested in theory as I had been. They wanted to know "how to use this stuff."

By any standards, I was a slow learner, but it is not the way I would recommend to others. If you want to be a fast learner, this book is for you. It is a book I wish I had had myself. It is an ASAP workbook.

It will work best as a supplement to spiritual activities such as Science of Mind classes and attending church on a regular basis. It is designed to satisfy the question, "How can I use these ideas in my daily life?"

I believe this workbook will also be useful as a review for people who think they already know it all because it provides a way of working on personal issues through journaling techniques which I first used as a writing teacher. Even if you think you have already mastered every idea in the book, you can still use these techniques to gain control over your thought patterns.

Any serious student of Science of Mind agrees that using principle depends on integrated understanding. And not everyone who thinks he/she understands principle really does. You don't have to be around long to hear people who should know better saying things such as, "I know God wants me to have that Cadillac." or "Well, God sent me this broken leg as a lesson in patience."

People come to Science of Mind churches and they like what they hear. If they stick around long enough to take classes and study principle, they do learn the theoretical basis of the teaching. If they take workshops and seminars, they will learn some practical applications for their daily lives. Science of Mind not only works but it works quickly for the serious student. Perhaps the greatest joy of the ministry is seeing the changes in the lives of people who study Science of Mind.

Some people don't stay long enough to give Science Of Mind a chance. I hope this book will help them stick around longer since it is simply written and can be used by anyone, anywhere.

Through years of study and thought, I have come to believe that Science of Mind offers answers to all life issues. While some of the ideas are simple, I don't believe it is possible to "outgrow" Science of Mind because there is always more to learn, and our understanding continues to deepen with sincere studies.

Despite the effectiveness and power of Science of Mind, many people fail to pursue their studies. There are five main reasons for this:

1. They don't want to change. (They unconsciously or consciously believe that the payoff for keeping the status quo is too great to risk any change at all.)
2. They haven't been able to understand Science of Mind principles as they were explained in lectures or class.
3. They don't believe in the Science of Mind teaching.
4. They don't believe in themselves enough to think they can change.
5. They don't know how to apply principle in their own lives. This book should be a major help in four out of five situations. It is written in simple, practical language. It is designed to give specific steps for people who want to practice the steps which lead to self confidence and conviction.

Practice is the key word. Most people are willing to read and grasp the surface of new ideas but only a few are willing to put the time and energy into practice which will really pay off. Please understand that the ideas you encounter here can change your life if you will take the time to work through the exercises.

This is a workbook - designed to be worked with - not read and discarded. As a former classroom teacher, I was familiar with the concept of practice workbooks or skills books which accompany textbooks. Whether the subject is composition, history, English, mathematics, or Science of Mind, lessons must be internalized and reflected through one's own consciousness before they are really learned.

You will want to work with this skills book over a period of time and actively engage in the exercises as you read. I suggest you keep a special notebook with your answers, essays and notes. I like to have some blank pages for drawings as well as lined paper. Date everything because it is interesting to look back and see your growth as well as refresh your mind.

Use the affirmations in your daily life. You may want to copy them out on 3x5 cards and carry them with you. Some of the shorter ones can be used as a mantra when you meditate. The treatments are there to be used. I find it effective to read treatments out loud - perhaps several times a day. Copy the ones you especially like and carry them with you.

When you are working with these lessons, be as honest as you can. There is a difference between changing your thinking and denying your feelings.

As you work with Science of Mind ideas, you will be making an attempt to change your thinking but there is no value in pretending to be somewhere you are not. So tell today's truth. The only place to begin a journey is where you are now.

Your work can be the most fascinating work you will ever do. You are embarking on a study of the grammar of your soul. The rewards for puncturing the mysteries of your mind will be astounding.

It is wonderful to see instant results and I believe you will quickly achieve many surprises if you apply this teaching to your life. I also believe that your commitment to Science of Mind should be a life-long commitment.

After the initial flush of success and the easy gains, you may not see the immediate rewards you hope for. Some issues take a long time to work through but they can be healed, released, de-fused or changed. Don't get discouraged.

You have a right to a good life. You have achieved the level of understanding which brought you into contact with this material, therefore, you must be ready. Approach it joyfully and learn to sing as you work. Life is beautiful.

LESSON ONE

SIMPLE TO UNDERSTAND - A CHALLENGE TO LIVE BY

To say that one can change his life by changing his thinking is exciting and stimulating. To actually begin to attempt to change one's thinking can be challenging. Practice doesn't exactly make perfect because we are all already perfect. However, practice uncovers and expresses perfect in desirable ways.

Learning to see through the perspective of Science of Mind is a long term process which is worth the effort. It takes a while and the progress is gradual but there will come a time when your understanding of spiritual principles is so strong that no external event can sway you or frighten you. You will never need to feel weak, helpless or afraid again.

Some students of Science of Mind will attain a level of conviction which enables them to have a life without any trouble at all. All our relationships can be loving, we can have plenty of money, excellent health and creative activities. We can really know the truth that sets us free.

Why do some of us find it so difficult to carry what we learn in classes and Sunday services into our daily life? Is Science of Mind too difficult for the average person? Does it only work for people who have college degrees? Or is it useful for emotional problems but silly when it comes to germs? These are some of the ideas you hear expressed by Science of Mind dropouts. Even some of our most devoted students can be heard to whine, "Why is it so hard to understand?"

Science of Mind is not difficult to understand. The basic ideas have been around for thousands of years and a working intellectual understanding can be grasped in about an hour.

We teach that we live in a spiritual universe and that the nature of that universe is Mind. We teach that Mind is creative and that our thought is creating our experience. We teach that we can change our lives by changing our thinking. These ideas can be found in children's books, fairy tales, and women's magazines as well as philosophy or physics.

The difficulty doesn't really lie in understanding basic principles, it lies in the practice of controlling our thoughts and learning to stop looking at the world through earth colored spectacles.

An appropriate analogy would be our million dollar diet industry. A second grader or functional illiterate can understand the basic concept of calories in, energy out. Understanding nutrition takes no more than a third grade education, yet many people who understand the laws well enough continue to eat apple pie for breakfast and complain that they can't lose weight.

For many, losing weight is difficult but not because they can't understand nutritional laws. It is difficult because they have yet to achieve the degree of commitment, desire or faith that the process of employing these laws requires.

Nutritional laws, like spiritual laws, operate whether there is anyone out there understanding them or not. Change comes when the eater begins to take control of her/his life by making conscious choices. For some, the work is easy, for others, the work is difficult but not because the laws change or can't be understood.

When a person achieves a degree of understanding which enables her/him to continually see the world as spiritually based and to constantly stay in touch with the fact that his/her life is God expressing, we often describe that person as enlightened. It is possible for anyone to experience a degree of understanding which might be called enlightenment, at least part of the time.

Enlightenment is usually a gradual process but anyone can move in the direction of enlightenment a day at a time. None of us has anything better to do with her/his life.

Days, months or years can pass before we can actually control our thinking well enough to construct a complete life which totally suits us but we immediately sense that Science of Mind, once mastered, is the path toward that kind of freedom.

Freedom is our natural birthright but we must be willing to change our way of looking at the world in order to attain it. True freedom is rare enough that we might describe it as a revolutionary state of being. Therefore, as you work with Science of Mind principles to claim your natural birthright of freedom, you can think of yourself as a spiritual revolutionary. You are important to the world which is on the cutting edge of a spiritual revolution.

The truth which we teach is simple enough but the results we find in our lives are revolutionary in the profoundest meaning of the word. You are in a position to make a real difference to yourself, to your community, your nation and this planet. You do make a difference.

Resistance is natural. You will encounter cultural ideas which need to be released and you will also encounter your own psychology which can be healed.

Never be discouraged as you attempt to employ this wonderful teaching in your life. It is natural that you will encounter resistance to changing your beliefs, especially when you first start your studies. Think of yourself as embarking on a program of mental exercises; as you practice, you develop mental muscles. Think of yourself as embarking on a program of learning a new language. Immersion and dedication bring fast results. Stick to your work and you will profit. You cannot fail.

We teach that we live in a spiritual world and that there are laws which are constant, and dependable. We say that you can use these laws to control your life and your experience. When we say things such as, "I am cause to my experience," or "Change your thinking and change your life," it is easy to dismiss the statements as nice ideas. Actually, we believe that each of us is really cause to his or her experience. We also believe that any condition, circumstance, feeling or environment can be changed by changing your thoughts. That is because we believe that your thoughts are creative in the same way that God or Universal Power is creative.

Many people attend church for a number of weeks, months or years and never really approach this truth. They enjoy the positive feelings they have while they are in church. They may even believe that the minister is a nice person who believes what he/she says. For some, Religious Science is the church of positive thinking. Beyond that, they continue to experience their world as a place *which happens at them* and they may use Science of Mind principles to help them cope. That's fine, but there is more to life than coping. There is a peace which passes understanding available to each and every one of us.

Once you have been exposed to Science of Mind, you have the key to freedom, health, wealth, joy and genius. It is simply a matter of working with your thought patterns long enough to change your basic belief systems. No one can do it for you and you probably can't do it in a day - but it can be done.

I believe the best way to use Science of Mind effectively is to immerse yourself in study and practice until it becomes second nature to you. Expecting one hour at church on Sunday to do the trick is expecting a lot of yourself and your minister.

In the end, you are your own best teacher. You are choosing to be here and you are choosing to change. Honor the teacher within yourself and listen carefully to the assignments which come from within. You have the power. You are the glory.

SKILL BUILDERS

1. Make a list of ten accomplishments you are proud of.
2. Circle those which took a systematic program of action.
3. List three things in your life you have already changed and are proud of.
4. Divide a paper into four parts and write one of these words in each square. Health, Love, Wealth, Creativity. Now rate yourself in terms of current success. Give one square a #1 for tops and one square a #2 etc. No ties allowed.
5. Look at your rating chart and ask yourself if you are surprised. Now list two or three changes you would make if you felt you could in each of the four

squares. Remember that the purpose of this exercise is to know oneself better - not to feel shame or discouragement. This is the first lesson - simply an assessment of where you are.

AFFIRMATIONS

...I love myself as I am and I am ready to make changes.
...I am light.
...I am love.
...I am joy.
...I am rich.
...I am health.

TREATMENT

I know that I live in a Universe which is constantly changing and creating new experiences. I know that I am a part of that Universe and that my new thoughts direct the Universe to create new experiences for me.

I now choose my thoughts carefully. I choose to think of health. I choose to think of wealth. I choose to think of love. I choose to think of creative enterprises.

If a thought of fear, worry, or despair comes to me, I quickly replace it with a positive one. I am in control of my life because I am in control of my thoughts.

I know that this treatment now enters the Universal Creative Mind and changes take place immediately in my experience. I release these words, knowing that positive changes are already taking place. And so it is.

LESSON TWO

YOU HAVE CHOICES

The most important lesson to learn is that you have choices. For example, when you pick up this book you have many choices.

..... You can choose not to buy the book.

..... You can buy it and choose not to read it.

.....You can skim through it and decide you already know everything that is in it, overlooking the possibility that you may not know how to practice everything you know.

..... You can read it quickly and give it to someone you think needs it more than you do.

......You can study it and write all your answers on scraps of paper and lose them quickly.

.....You can study the book and struggle over each lesson for months, using the book as another way to feel like a failure.

.....You can study it and get some changes in your life and then take up a different spiritual teaching such as belly dancing or automatic writing.

.....You can study this book and do the lessons for as long as it takes you to fully integrate the lessons into your life.

.....You can use the book over and over, for the rest of your life. Since the important material comes from your reactions, the book will deepen and grow more profound as your understanding grows.

There are as many scenarios as there are individuals who come into contact with the Science of Mind teaching. Each of us is a unique individual.

We all have hundreds of opportunities to make new choices each day. Your choice to read this far in this book can pay off greatly for you. Books do change lives and this one will work for you. Please remember that total immersion in your new way of thinking will bring spectacular results.

The best ways to build a pattern of success is to pay attention to the choices you are making and the results you see. Form the habit of keeping a record of your treatments and the results. You may wish to use the same journal you are using for Science of Mind Skills or you may keep notes in your daytimer.

It is important to keep a record of your spiritual progress. This will build your consciousness and your conviction. Reinforce your learning as much as you can. You will certainly want to be going to church on a regular basis. You will also want to read other books and listen to tapes to improve your theoretical understanding of Science of Mind.

There is an old saying that when the student is ready the teacher appears. There is also a spiritual truth that tells us we have everything we need to know within ourselves. This book is a key to unlock the treasures you already own. You can choose to be both student and teacher with the help of this book. Choose wisely. You are ready to change.

SKILL BUILDERS

1. Select your method of keeping track of your treatments and the results. You may use a notebook, or computer file but make sure you keep your notes together.
2. Make a list of ten positive choices you have made recently.
3. Make a list of ten positive choices you plan to make this week.

AFFIRMATIONS

...I trust life.
...I trust myself.
...I always know the right choice to make.
...My life is divinely guided.
...I do have choices.
...I choose the best for myself.

TREATMENT

Divine Intelligence, which has guided me this far, now supplies all that I need to make intelligent choices for this day. I choose rightly and well since I am guided by Divine Intelligence.

I face this day without fear. As challenges arise, as issues need to be resolved, as choices appear, I know exactly what to do. I need not hesitate. I need not worry. I am in my right place, making right decisions. Right action is easy for me.

I rely on Divine Intelligence to bring whatever is necessary into view so that I make intelligent choices. I trust myself and I trust Divine Intelligence. And so it is.

LESSON THREE

IN THE NAME OF GOD

As a child, you may have learned that the word God meant a large, angry giant who was watching you from a distance. Not only does Science of Mind say that God is not angry, but God is also not a person - large or small.

Disassociating yourself from the idea that God is punishing or judging you is important if you are to accomplish anything in your Science of Mind studies. One way to understand these new ideas is to use a different vocabulary for First Cause - that Creative Process which humans have defined as God.

As you progress in your studies, you will learn more and more about the nature of God and you will discover that you can develop your own words to describe your own definition of what the magnificent power you are using can be called.

In the beginning, it will be helpful to become familiar with some of the synonyms which we use for the title of God. These synonyms hint at a broader, more enlightened definition that you will want to enlarge upon in time as you continue your spiritual studies.

Here are some of the interchangeable terms for God which Science of Mind teachers use. In your reading you may discover others. Usually, writers will capitalize words to give you an indication of their divine meaning.

God, First Cause, Creative Process, Divine Intelligence, Divine Mind, Divine Givingness, Infinite Intelligence, Infinite Wisdom, Creative Power, Universal

Power, Higher Power, Father, Father-Mother God, and One are all used to designate the same thing.

Often, in this book, you will find the word Universe used as a synonym because it seems to have the fewest connotations for people. Even if you believe you are allergic to religion and the word God, you can use affirmations with the word Universe in them and not have a reaction. Try it.

SKILL BUILDERS

1. Write a sentence using each of the synonyms used above. Make the sentence an affirmative claim. Example - "Divine Mind now produces a great job for me."
2. Put a star beside the words which seem to work best for you at this time.
3. Write a paragraph describing your image of God today. Date it and keep it.

AFFIRMATIONS

...I now have a great relationship with the Universe.
...Universal Intelligence guides and protects me.
...I am surrounded by Universal Love.

TREATMENT

One Life, One God, One Power.

I consciously connect with that Universal Power which surrounds and supports me in my positive actions and I allow myself to be helped in new and wonderful ways.

I depend on Universal Power to accomplish what I want to have accomplished. I depend on the Universe to supply love, health, wealth, joy, and happiness. I know that I am supported and surrounded by an Infinite Wisdom which is in a positive relationship to me and my life.

I rest assured that all is well and so it is.

LESSON FOUR

YOUR RELATIONSHIP TO GOD

You were created in the image and likeness of God because God is creative and you are creative. Not only do you live, move and have your being in God, but you use your mind to create as God.

While this is a difficult concept for many beginners to grasp completely, you will become familiar with the process of your creating activities through your studies and eventually begin to understand it in a new way.

Religious Science is a teaching which helps people use their God-given power more efficiently and intelligently. In order to do that well, we have to give up some of the old ideas we have used and begin to use new ideas more definitely. One place to begin is in our thinking about our relationship to God.

As you learned in the previous lesson, in Science of Mind, we use many different names for that Creative Process which you have heard called God. This terminology helps us understand our true relationship to Infinite Life.

Some teachers never use the word God at all because there are so many old, out-moded ideas surrounding the word that they prefer to use other terminology to help their students free themselves from outmoded thinking.

Basically, Religious Science teaches that God is all there is and therefore, we each live within God. This is a very different concept than the old idea that God is a very large and powerful personage who is outside of us and judging everything we do.

Fear of God is not a part of Religious Science thinking but many students begin their work with a lot of guilt, fear or anxiety about their relationship with God. Sometimes it is better to use one of the other terms for God when you are doing your prayer treatments and studying your lessons because it helps you free yourself from worn out ideas.

Since God is all there is, God can surely have many names. Since God is all wise, Divine Intelligence is a good, useful name. Since God is all powerful, Universal Power is another good name for God. Since God is love, Divine Love is another useful term. Since God is the First Cause and the Source and Infinite Intelligence - Infinite Power, Infinite Wisdom and Infinite Intelligence are all good names.

I like to use the name Creative Process because it describes the creative nature of God and insinuates the ability to change conditions rapidly. Some people who come out of 12 Step Programs may continue to use the words Higher Power.

Be careful not to fall into titles or names which make God less than all powerful, all wise, and everywhere present. Don't refer to God as having a human nature or gender. Terms such as "The man upstairs," may indicate a lack of fear but they limit our conception of God.

Many people are comfortable with phrases such as Father/Mother God or The Father Within because they believe it enhances their sense of closeness to The Source. Use phrases which are comfortable to you only if you are truly clear that you are dealing with an Omnipotent One, not an identity outside yourself.

SKILL BUILDERS

1. Write a short paragraph describing the way you saw God as a child. What were your earliest reactions to the idea of God? Were they favorable or frightening?
2. List any attributes which you thought belonged to God as a child which you still believe in.
3. List any ideas you had about God as a child which no longer serve you.
4. Make a new list based on the previous two. Replace old ideas that do not represent Truth and keep (or rephrase) the ones which still seem right. For example, I thought *God was a big Santa Claus in the sky*. Might become *God does give us what we can accept*. And it also might become *God is not distant but right here and now in my life*.

AFFIRMATIONS

...*I live, move and have my being in God.*
...*God is present everywhere, present right here and now.*
...*God is a Universal Power for Good which is with me always.*
...*God and I are One.*

TREATMENT

One God, One Mind, One Universal Force. I am immersed in that wonderful Divine Mind. I am supported by Divine Intelligence and I am surrounded by Divine Love.

I know that the power of the Universe is behind my words because of my connection with my source. All that is necessary is for me to accept the gifts of Spirit which I now claim.

At this very moment, I claim a more definite and complete understanding of my relationship to God. This understanding immediately reveals itself in increased health, increased wealth, increased love and increased wisdom.

There is only God in my life and I discard all old, outmoded ideas about having to earn God's love. I can never be separated from my Source. I accept my new understanding of God and I accept the fact that I am God's love expressing itself through my life. I accept this new wisdom and I trust life more than ever before. I let this treatment go - knowing that the work has already been done in the mind of God and so it is.

LESSON FIVE

A SPIRITUAL UNIVERSE

We live in a spiritual universe, ruled by a creative intelligence. There is a pattern of law and love which we can rely upon. We sometimes call this patterned intelligence - God and sometimes we call it Divine Intelligence.

Divine Intelligence is constantly surrounding and supporting us. Because of our lack of understanding, we may sometimes feel alone or separated from God but the truth is that God is all there is and God is always there. Therefore, we can never be separated from our Infinite Source.

SKILL BUILDERS

1. Ask yourself when you have felt closest to God. Write a short paragraph describing the situation and how you felt. Try to recreate the feeling and remember it.
2. If you cannot remember a specific time when you felt close to God, remember a time when you were very, very happy. Write about that feeling. You can use it to do the following exercises.
3. This day, make a conscious decision to recall and recreate that feeling of closeness at least three more times. If you were madly in love with someone, you would be thinking about that person during your day. To fall in love with God is to have a permanent feeling of bliss.
4. Write down your experiences of remembering.

5. At the end of the day make some notes about the effectiveness of your work. Did you notice any changes in your attitude toward others? Did anything go better than usual? How do you feel now? Have you made any discoveries about your relationship to God?

AFFIRMATIONS

...God and I are one.
...I am surrounded and supported by God's love.
...I am made in the image and likeness of God.
...I celebrate my Godness.

TREATMENT

One Mind, One Power, One God. I am connected to, immersed in, surrounded by that God Power. I live, move and have my being in God.

Right now, I make a conscious decision to open myself to a greater understanding of my connection to God than I have ever had before. I drop all old, outmoded ideas about the nature of God which no longer serve me. I drop fear. I drop shame. I drop guilt. I drop awe. I allow myself to know the truth which sets me free.

I am a living expression of God. Nothing about me is foreign to God or unacceptable to that Divine Presence. While it is true I am in the process of becoming all that I can be, it is also true that I already am everything that I could ever want to be. At the level of God's truth, I am perfect, whole and complete. I allow myself to know that - really know that - now.

I know that every treatment I do makes a shift in my understanding and awareness and I know that this is a powerful, direct treatment which focuses my awareness on the truth of my being. God and I are One and I know it. And so it is!

LESSON SIX

SPIRIT IS THE BASIS OF ALL LIFE

Creative Energy or Spirit is the basis of all life. Spirit is back of every form and experience which we call life. Our thoughts give direction to Creative Energy which produces forms and experiences.

While we are unique and individualized expressions of this Spirit, we are not separate from it. We are immersed in Spirit. We have the ability to direct Creative Energy to produce experiences.

Science of Mind is a study of what life really is and how to direct our thoughts to produce experiences which we want to have. As we gain understanding of our spiritual nature and the spiritual nature of the universe, we gain control over our lives.

SKILL BUILDERS

1. Make a list of positive things which you have thought about in the past or envisioned which have come into your life.
2. Take a look at other people you know and see how their belief systems appear to be controlling their experiences.
3. Make a list of beliefs you wish you held. For example, you may wish you believed, "I am lucky."
4. Think of ways your belief system has already expanded since you were first introduced to positive thinking or Science of Mind.

AFFIRMATIONS

...*What I can believe, I can achieve.*

...*I expect the best in my life.*

...*I am always looking on the bright side.*

TREATMENT

One Mind, One Power, One God. God is present everywhere, at all times - present right here and now. I am immersed in God. I live, move and have my being in God. I am one with God.

I now choose to allow all false beliefs, all outmoded, old fashioned, no longer useful ideas to melt away. I choose to think only positive, constructive thoughts. I choose the best for myself.

I know that God is on my side, supporting me in this decision, If God is with me, who can be against me? I expect the best from this moment forward and I am willing to let the best come into full view in my life right now. And so it is.

LESSON SEVEN

YOUR MESSAGE CENTER

Your thoughts act as constant messages to Universal Mind. You are creating an atmosphere of thoughts which surround you and bring experiences into your life. For example, if you believe you are unlucky, you are surely attracting trouble into your life.

The thoughts which surround you create something which is called a "mental atmosphere". It is something like the eastern concept of an aura although you won't necessarily see it but it does surround you and consistently sends messages to the Universe.

Much of the work you will be doing in this book is aimed at creating a more pleasing mental atmosphere. You can lighten up your thought system and that will lighten up your life.

SKILL BUILDERS

1. Today make it a point to notice what you are usually thinking about other people. Jot down notes in your notebook. Don't make judgments, simply observe.
2. Make it a point to notice what you are usually thinking about yourself today. Jot down some of the messages you are sending to the Universe about yourself. For example, do you find yourself thinking, "I am stupid," or "I am smart."

3. Take a look at the messages you are sending the Universe about other people. Are there things you'd like to change? How? Write it down.

4. Take a look at the messages you are sending the Universe about yourself. Are there things you'd like to change? How? Write it down?

5. Generally speaking, are you harder on yourself or others? Would you like to treat yourself as well as others? The Golden Rule works both ways. How would it feel to love yourself as much as others? What would change in your life?

AFFIRMATIONS

...I love myself.
...I think the best about myself.
...I think the best about others.
...I am teachable.
...I am willing and able to improve my self image.

TREATMENT

I know that there is a Power For Good in the universe and I am using it. My thoughts are directive thoughts and my prevailing thought patterns are positive and loving. I love myself and recognize the beauty and joy that lives within me.

I know that no matter what I have done in the past, no matter what has been done to me in the past, I have never been damaged. I can never be damaged because I am perfect whole and complete - made in the image and likeness of God.

While there may be conditions, emotions or experiences in my life which I now choose to change, I know that there is nothing about my essential nature which needs to be changed nor could it ever be changed. I live, move and have my being in God. I am God's living enterprise. I am a beautiful, intelligent, wonderful person right here and now. I accept this truth and my acceptance of this truth allows me to express my perfection in new and wonderful ways. And so it is.

LESSON EIGHT

YOU ARE THE DIRECTOR

One of the first things to understand is that you are constantly directing Creative Energy (God or Spirit) to provide new experiences in your life. Every time you say, "I am..."(and really accept it) the words act as an order which the Universe will find a way to fulfill.

SKILL BUILDERS
1. Make a list of ten attributes with which you wish to identify.
2. Take that list with you today and read it aloud several times. Each time you read the list, try and create a feeling of conviction. Your voice will show you the way.
3. If you hear yourself saying something negative about yourself, stop and correct yourself immediately. Imagine that you have a mental eraser and you can erase the thought. For example, change, "I am old," to "I am eternal life - vigorous, joyful and young."
4. When you see someone who has something you would like, make a mental identification immediately. Don't waste your time on envy. Spend your time imagining yourself having whatever you want. You can, you know!
5. If anyone gives you a compliment today, thank them and repeat it so that you can be sure that it sinks into your consciousness. For instance, if your friend

says, "That's a pretty dress," you can say, "Thank you. I'm glad you like my dress. Red is my favorite color."

6. Make a special effort to say something nice about yourself today. If it isn't appropriate to say anything to other people, stand in front of the mirror and say, "I am a good person," or whatever. But don't be too shy. There is power in saying to your best friend, "I am good at mathematics." You don't need agreement for your words to have power.

7. At the end of the day review your work. Did you feel uncomfortable praising yourself? Did you like really hearing any compliments? Do you really believe your thoughts are causing your experience? If not, what do you believe?

AFFIRMATIONS

...The power of the Universe is behind my prayer treatments.

...I am not a victim, I create my own experience.

...My thoughts are powerful and positive.

TREATMENT

Divine Intelligence guides and supports me as I move through this day. I know that my thoughts are creating a new and wonderful reality for me. I use the full force of my connection to Divine Intelligence to bring positive new experiences into my life quickly.

There is no situation or condition which presents a challenge to Divine Intelligence. Divine Intelligence always finds a way, always overcomes an obstacle, always melts an emotion, always resolves a conflict when I allow it to do so.

I now allow my actions and thoughts to be the highest and best. I allow myself to expect the best and this is evident in my conversation and in my actions. I allow myself to accept the best, knowing that I am a living expression of God and worthy of all the best.

I accept perfect health, I accept great wealth, I accept love, I accept exciting new opportunities, I accept the best right now. And so it is.

LESSON NINE

YOU ARE ATTRACTIVE

You attract things you pay attention to. Anything you focus on, you will probably get more of. For instance, if you count your money and you say, "I have so much money!" there is a good chance that you will attract more money. If you look at the pimple on the end of your nose and say, "I hate this pimple! Why do I have this pimple?" chances are good that you will get more pimples.

The law of attraction is always working and you can learn to use this law as a tool to achieve whatever you want. Begin to pay attention to the things and experiences you want in your life. It will pay off.

SKILL BUILDERS

1. Make a list of experiences which seem to come easy to you. For instance, it may be easy for you to make friends or it may be easy for you to grow flowers.
2. Divide the list into experiences you want more of and those you want less of.
3. Make it a point to mention those things you want at least once a day for one week. Keep a record of any results you think you notice. For example, if you say, "I make friends easily," and at the end of the week, you have two new friends, write it down.

4. Make it a point not to mention the things you don't want to attract. For instance, if you are experiencing arthritis in your knees, don't mention it all week and make note of the results.

AFFIRMATIONS

...*I am a money magnet.*
...*I attract wonderful people into my life.*
...*I am surrounded by love.*
...*I am the picture of health.*
...*Positive new experiences come into my life.*

TREATMENT

There is one wonderful Power operating in life and that Power is working in my life now. I know that the Power of The Universe backs this treatment and that my words bring immediate, definite results.

I claim only the very best for myself from this moment forward. I claim a great deal of wealth, excellent health, great relationships, a loving life, and wonderful creative enterprises as mine, right now. I know that Universal Mind knows only this moment and there need be no delays in response to my claims.

As I can accept, I can receive. I now accept the very best for myself. I accept it right now. I expect it right now. I open my mind, my heart and my eyes to the possibilities of life. I look to this day, for it is Life. And so it is.

LESSON TEN

POWER NOW

Many people confuse the ideas they find in Science of Mind with psychological ideas about positive thinking.

While it is true that Science of Mind treatments and affirmations often work on the psychological level of the person receiving the treatment, it is not limited to that.

For example, if a salesman does a treatment for higher sales figures, and he believes in the efficacy of the treatment, his psychological attitude will change and he will probably make more sales.

However, the treatment does much more than simply affect the mental attitude the salesperson, it directs Divine Mind to produce results which may take many different forms. More customers come to the store, the commission level may be raised, and there can be an opportunities or promotions which the salesperson doesn't imagine when he is treating.

Science of Mind is not positive thinking or self hypnosis or psychological counseling. It is a system for actually changing experiences by changing the instructions we are giving to God.

Because Science of Mind is so effective, results sometimes appear to be miraculous. However, there is nothing miraculous involved because the results are based on spiritual laws which are always working.

SKILL BUILDERS

1. Make a list of events and experiences which you have seen happen or have happened to you which appeared miraculous.

2. Make a list of events and experiences which you hope to see which would seem like miracles.

3. Take the events in the second list and change them into affirmations. For instance, if you have listed that you'd like to sell your house, write an affirmation, "This house is now sold for a good price to the perfect person."

4. Imagine at least one situation in which changing your psychological attitude would help you achieve results. Write a paragraph describing those results as though they had already happened. Write in the present tense.

AFFIRMATIONS

...*Life is my miracle.*

...*There is nothing supernatural about health, wealth and happiness.*

...*I am in tune psychologically, physically and spiritually.*

TREATMENT

I know that the Universe supports me, surrounds me, and supplies me. I am now perfectly at home with the truth of my nature - that I am at one with God.

I use this knowledge of my oneness with God to create great changes in my current life. I allow myself to change any behaviors that no longer suit me. I allow myself to change any beliefs that no longer serve me. I allow myself to love and be loved. I allow myself to express health and wealth. I allow myself to live fully, without restriction, without reservation. The truth has set me free. I am at one with God and I am at one with myself. For we are one and the same. And so it is.

LESSON ELEVEN

YOU ARE RESPONSIBLE

Science of Mind places responsibility for life in the lap of each individual because it teaches that we are creating our own experience. When people first encounter this idea, they sometimes think that the appropriate reaction is to blame themselves for being ill or unhappy or lonely. This is not correct.

Understanding that we are responsible is the first step to freedom. The more quickly we let go of the idea of self-blame or self-punishment, the more quickly we can accomplish our goals. It is important to remember that whatever we pay attention to is what we are telling the Universe we want more of. Therefore, if you are experiencing a broken ankle and you wish to experience a complete healing, you must focus on health, not illness.

Searching for the reason behind the act of breaking your ankle may sometimes be helpful but it is not the same as healing the ankle. Looking for a diagnosis is not creating a sound body. Spend your time and energy thinking about what you want, not worrying about what you don't want. Divine Intelligence provides whatever you ask for. Every time you are thinking about something, you are (in a way) asking for it.

SKILL BUILDERS

1. Select one current experience you consider negative and begin by "owning" it. For example, if you are constantly broke, say to yourself, "I created this shortage."

2. Make a short list of possible reasons you might have created the experience. For example, "I wanted to avoid working too hard," or "I spend a lot to have something good in my life," or "I didn't get that promotion because the boss is just like my father who was mean to me when I was little."

3. Look at your reasons and laugh. Or if you are not ready to laugh at them cross them off one by one and write positive affirmations to replace them.

4. Decide whether you are willing to let go of the experience today.

5. If you decide to hold onto the experience a while longer, say out loud, "I have a right to make choices and I am choosing to hold onto this _____ today. I know I can make a new choice tomorrow."

6. If you decide to let go of the experience, say, "I have a right to make new choices and I am choosing to let go of this experience today. No matter what my reasons for creating it were, I am willing to find new ways to fulfill those needs. This condition has served me in the past but it no longer serves me. I bless and release it now."

7. Make a list of ways in which you may choose to fulfill your needs. For example, if spending money has been used for nurturing, list other ways to nurture yourself such as taking naps or taking time to exercise or listening to music every day.

8. Watch your thinking carefully today and mentally erase any thoughts which are not self loving. For example, if you catch yourself thinking, "I walk like an old lady with this broken ankle," immediately erase the thought by saying decisively, "I am eternal youth, vigorous and powerful." Say it with conviction.

AFFIRMATIONS

...I have wonderful choices.
...I am responsible for my life.
...There is a spiritual basis for my life.
...I choose to love myself.
...I choose to be the best me I can.
...I can never be a victim of circumstance because I create my circumstances.
...The power resides in me. I choose my experience.

TREATMENT

One Mind, One Creative Power, One Divine Intelligence, One God. I am having my life within that which is all there is - God.

My life is God's life and no harm can come to me. Nothing but love, goodness and mercy can follow from God.

I know that any negative experience I am having is simply nothing in the eyes of God. I am perfect, whole and complete right now, in the past and in the future. I accept full responsibility for any situation in my life which expresses less than that perfection, that completeness and that wholeness. I now choose to let go of all false beliefs, all old behavior patterns or negative emotions which may have held that experience in place.

I let it go. I light a candle of wisdom in the darkness of former ignorance. I let go and let God. I bless and release. I move on - expressing more life and light than ever before. I am alive in the truth of God and so it is.

LESSON TWELVE

PRAYER TREATMENT

Science of Mind has a special vocabulary which you may have heard but may not really understand. Do you know the difference between a prayer and a treatment?

Basically, a treatment is like a prayer in that you are talking to God. However, it is different because you are not asking or pleading for a gift, you are going through mental steps which will allow you to accept and claim the gift.

You can do this because everything in the universe is made up of Divine Intelligence or what most people call God. But that God is not a person, place or thing; it is a creative process. You are part of that God and you can direct your experience.

Treatment is an organized system for setting creative process into motion. It isn't very different from thinking except it is direct, focused and organized.

Treatment is called treatment instead of prayer because early New Thought teachers wanted to make sure that everyone understood that a spiritual mind treatment was a healing command, not a plea for mercy.

SKILL BUILDERS

1. Make a list of five things you would like to treat for.
2. Write each of those things into a present tense, affirmative statement. For example, "I have new roller skates."
3. Imagine yourself as a healer who is carrying a black bag. Imagine yourself walking into your own room and seeing yourself sitting in a chair. Carry on an imaginary conversation between yourself as a healer and yourself as a client. Jot down notes of the interchange.

AFFIRMATIONS

...Life is a treat.

...I am healing myself now.

...My life is healthy and happy and well.

...I am Wisdom Itself.

TREATMENT

God is present here and now and God answers before I have asked the question. The answer is in the prayer itself. I ask and receive, thereby living out the Law and living out the Love.

I am connected to a wonderful Source which is always available, always reliable and which knows neither limitation nor time. There are no obstacles to my success. What I can conceive and believe, I do achieve.

My dreams come true. I am living in a wonderful world of abundance and plenty. I am loved and I am love. All my relationships are positive and getting better. I attract more and more goodness to me. I am a magnet for success because I assume success is my birthright. I know that I am living out of my own personal vision and that I am supported in that vision by an omnipotent, omnipresent God.

Right now, I accept the very best. Riches, wisdom, love and health are now mine for I have spoken the word and Spirit rushes to fulfill my word. And so it is.

LESSON THIRTEEN

RECOGNIZING GOD

There are usually five steps in a treatment. The first one is recognition. In recognizing God, we are establishing the truth which will set us free. God is all there is; everywhere present, all powerful and all encompassing. God is Creative Action.

SKILL BUILDERS

1. Ask yourself what God looks like. Draw a picture or write a description.
2. Religious Science teaches that God is all there is. See if you can imagine the God you described as being all encompassing. Are you inside or outside of your God?
3. Does your concept of God need to be expanded? Can you see God as a creative process?
4. Practice knowing that God is all around and in you. Make sure that your God is a loving God.
5. Is there any healing necessary in your relationship to God? Do you need to see God in a new way so that God can see you in a new way?
6. Today, practice knowing that God is everywhere you go. See God in the grocery check-out line. See God in the face of every child you meet. See God when you look in the mirror.

7. Select some music you especially like and sit down or lie down and listen to the music. Let your mind dwell on the idea that God is all there is. Feel surrounded and supported by this idea.

AFFIRMATIONS

...God is all there is.

...God is present everywhere.

...There's not a spot where God is not.

...God surrounds and supports me at all times.

...God and I are co-creators of my life.

TREATMENT

I drink deeply in Wisdom's Well. Quenching my thirst with truth, letting the golden fluid of God's love flow through me. I am one with God and I know it.

My thirst is quenched. I am at rest. I am at peace with the sure and certain knowledge that I am living my life in eternal life. Nothing can ever harm me. Nothing can ever discourage me. Nothing can ever delay me. I am One. I am at Peace. I am in Love and so it is.

LESSON FOURTEEN

UNIFICATION OR IDENTIFICATION

The second step in treatment is called unification or identification. It is knowing that you are unified with God. Complete knowledge of this unification might earn you the label of enlightened. All mystic experiences are based on the knowledge of unity with God.

SKILL BUILDERS

1. Remember a time when you felt absolutely at peace and in harmony with the universe. Recreate that feeling in your mind. During the day, pull that feeling out of your memory bank and enjoy it.
2. Imagine what you could do if you were absolutely convinced that the Power of the Universe was behind your treatments. Make a list of what you choose to accomplish. The sky's the limit!
3. Select the three most important things on your list. Put stars beside them.
4. Select the three things on your list which seem most possible. Put checks beside them.
5. Take the starred and checked items and write affirmations beginning with the words, "I am." For example, if you listed world peace as one of your most important items, write, "I am peace."

6. Keep your affirmations with you for a few days and practice reading them aloud. Whatever you claim in mind can be accomplished. The words, "I am,' work like magic.

7. During the day, if you feel any sense of aloneness or fear, imagine yourself as being totally enclosed in a ball of white light. That light is God's light and you can choose whom to let into your circle. You have the power.

8. As you walk in crowded places, try and see each person as surrounded by his or her own circle of white light. See her/him as separate and unified at the same time. See yourself as protected by love.

9. Respond slowly to questions or other people's actions today. Make each of your responses as conscious and you can. Take time to feel centered and surrounded by God's love before you answer even simple questions about what you want or what you will do. You are in charge and God is your powerful ally.

10. See yourself as letting light stream through you. Know that you can not be diminished by giving but you have a choice about how to spend your time and energy. Let love and light flow mentally but don't try to "fix" anyone or anything.

11. Keep your own counsel. Don't dissipate the effectiveness of this work by telling others about it. Try not to make fun of yourself or what you are doing. This is the most important work you can be doing right now.

AFFIRMATIONS

...I am one with God.

...God and I are one.

...The Universe supports and surrounds me.

...Divine Intelligence provides for me and protects me.

...My nature is God's nature - peace, love and joy.

...God and I co-creators of my world.

...I am totally immersed in God's love.

...I am filled with light.

TREATMENT

Quickly, surely, I move toward the light. I let myself feel the closeness of God. I rest in love and peace and joy, knowing that I am surrounded by love, immersed in light and at peace with all.

I am filled with the peace which passes all understanding. I am filled with light. I am filled with love. I let this wonderful light spill over my boundaries and move out into the lives of my loved ones, my friends, my neighbors, my workplace, and my community. I am a candle which brings light wherever I go. My light shines brightly, warming all. And so it is.

LESSON FIFTEEN

I DECLARE

The third step of treatment is called declaration. It often takes the form of an affirmation, such as, "I am health", or "I am wealth."

Sometimes people ask what the difference is between a treatment and an affirmation. Affirmations are shortcut treatments which resemble the declarations in the third step of treatment. In both cases, you claim the idea, belief, item, feeling or whatever you want.

Most people find full treatments more effective than short affirmations because the process of a treatment builds conviction. It is the conviction which does the job, not the process. In other words, it is the content, not the form which is important in all mental work.

SKILL BUILDERS

1. Take your list of affirmations from yesterday and practice saying them out loud in a voice that makes a positive declaration.
2. Remember that your declarations are statements about what you are claiming in your life. Imagine you are sitting in a restaurant looking at a limitless menu. You are ordering off the menu of life in the Universe Cafe. What will you have? Make a new list.
3. Take your new list and write it in "I am" sentences. For example, "I am the owner of a brand new car."

4. Check to make sure all your declarations are in the present tense. Work with the idea, "I am," not, "I will be".

5. Make a treasure map. Write "I am" in the middle of a sheet of paper and paste pictures from magazines of what you are claiming for yourself.

6. Check your reactions to this declaration exercise. Are you comfortable claiming good feelings and things for yourself? Do you need to give yourself permission to claim the best for yourself?

7. Spend some quiet time imagining what you will feel like when you have declared yourself into a new life. Get into the good feelings and claim those good feelings right now. Take the list below or your own list and speak your word with great conviction. You can claim the best. You deserve the best!

AFFIRMATIONS

...*I deserve the best.*
...*I declare I am wonderful.*
...*I claim my happiness now.*
...*I claim health now.*
...*I claim wealth now.*
...*I claim joy now.*
...*I claim love now .*
...*I claim happiness now.*
...*I claim wonderful work now.*

TREATMENT

There is a Power For Good in the Universe and I am now using it in my life. I speak my word and it is so.

I speak my word right now for the best and the brightest of my dreams. I recognize that desire is a clue for fulfillment and I state my desires clearly and definitely at this time.

I claim:

_____

_____

_____

Having made my claims, I now release them to Divine Intelligence, knowing that the work is already done in Mind. I let go and let God. And so it is.

LESSON SIXTEEN

HANDLING OBJECTIONS

There are times when we are doing treatment work and we discover objections. These objections may be based on "common sense" or old thought patterns which haunt us. For instance, it may be difficult for me to say I am wealthy with conviction when "common sense" tells me I have a large debt on my credit card. Or I may be so accustomed to thinking of myself as unworthy of love because of abuse I suffered as a child, that it is difficult for me to say, "I am love".

Overcoming objections is important for a successful treatment because the work is not complete until you can really accept it. When objections lurk in the shadows of our mind, we cannot get completion. Usually, the way to overcome objections is to move beyond appearances and into spiritual truth. In other words, objections can usually be overcome by going back and thinking about the creative nature of God. Your declaration can be accomplished despite objections because God is all there is and God only knows good about us.

The reason Science of Mind is so effective and makes far more lasting and deeper changes in people's lives than self-help books or positive thinking programs is that Science of Mind is based on a true understanding of the nature and power of God. God is Universal Spirit which is forever creating new forms.

SKILL BUILDERS

1. Make a list of objections you may hold to claiming health now.
2. Make a list of objections you may hold to claiming wealth now.
3. Make a list of objections you may hold to claiming love now.
4. Make a list of objections you may hold to claiming creative expression now.
5. Go back and cross out the objections one by one. As you cross them out, say one or more of these statements aloud, with conviction.

   …With God all things are possible.

   … I know that God dissolves all past patterns and false beliefs.

   …There is no such thing as evil, failure or sin. God only sees the truth and the truth is the goodness of God.

   …Divine Intelligence knows the way to solve any problem.

   …There is no truth in this idea of disease (or poverty or whatever).

   …God is always creating new forms and nothing in the past is permanent or ordained for the future.

   ….God is not limited by time or space.

   ….God does not judge.

   ….God does not know big or small.

AFFIRMATIONS

…I am mastering Science of Mind Skills quickly and easily.

…I resonate to the truth and the truth sets me free now.

…The Power of the Universe is behind my current work.

…I am led to discover new power and new joy.

TREATMENT

I know that Divine Intelligence surrounds and supports my life and that all things are possible with God. I also know that I am directly connected to that Infinite Source of wisdom, truth, power and love called God.

Since I am in the flow of Divine Energy and Love, I can never be discouraged or frightened. I am always creating new experiences and events in my life and I am moving forward in my acceptance of more wealth, more health, more happiness and more love.

I have the patience it takes to open up to more good. I do not delay my choices by worry or doubt. I patiently and lovingly remind myself that God and I are One. I patiently push open the pipeline of acceptance within. I firmly and lovingly push out the barriers and obstacles in my belief system. I choose to change and I allow myself to change in a loving manner.

No matter how firmly fixed some situation may seem, I remind myself that Spirit is always creating new forms. I am willing to release the old and let in the new. I am willing to get better. I am willing to have better. I am willing to be better.

I am never discouraged. I know that God does not know time and that all time is now. I know that I allow myself whatever it takes to attain my vision. I remind myself gently to keep working on my acceptance of good and I do not waste my time or talent on false emotions such as fear, doubt or worry.

I am in the correct position and frame of mind to let change happen. I am ready to take any necessary steps to implement that change. I choose to keep working on my spiritual growth, knowing that change will manifest as I grow in understanding. I choose to grow in understanding right now. I let this be so and so it is.

LESSON SEVENTEEN

I ACCEPT THE BEST

Acceptance is the fourth step in treatment. In order for a spiritual mind treatment to work, the person for whom the treatment is intended must be willing to accept it. We are all constantly working on opening our acceptance level. Long after we understand principle, we are opening up to more and more good.

SKILL BUILDERS

1. Imagine an hourglass and see yourself as the neck in the hourglass. Now imagine spirit giving gifts which must pass through the neck of the hourglass to take form.
2. Draw a picture of the hourglass. Put your name on the neck.
3. Widen the neck of the hourglass with your pencil. That is a picture of how your work is done. Spirit is always willing to give the gift, it is our acceptance which we are changing.

AFFIRMATIONS

...I accept more and more.
...I accept myself as whole, perfect and complete.
...I accept Christmas every day.
...I have an acceptance mentality.

...My acceptance is so great I wake each morning with joy.
...The purpose of my days is to collect the gifts of Spirit.

TREATMENT

I know that there is a Power For Good which is greater than I am and that this Power is working in my life now.

My vision is established in Divine Mind. I know exactly what I want and I know that I will be led to exactly the right steps in order to bring my vision into being on the relative plane of experience. I am willing to do whatever is necessary and I am willing to let the vision unfold in any way which is appropriate.

I accept my vision wholeheartedly right now. My goals are established and my expectation is of the best. I accept the best and the best comes to me quickly and easily. And so it is.

LESSON EIGHTEEN

LET GO AND LET GOD

The last step in any treatment is called release. You cannot plant a seed and then dig it up every hour to see how it is growing. You should not do a treatment and then worry all day about whether or not it is working.

In time, you will get so good at treatment work that you will probably be able to actually "feel" a shift in consciousness when the work is done. In the beginning, treat until you feel you have mentally accepted the desired result and say, "I release this treatment to Divine Intelligence".

SKILL BUILDERS

1. Pick something you have been working with for a long time. Do a treatment.
2. Release the treatment.
3. Every time you think about that issue for this week, say, "I have already done my work on this. Divine Mind now brings it into form."

AFFIRMATIONS

...Divine Mind always knows the way to accomplish anything.
...Divine Mind is now working for me on this issue.
...I let go and let God.

TREATMENT

Divine Intelligence, which has guided me so far, is now supplying everything which is necessary in order to establish my goals. I have envisioned the best and it now comes into being by simple and easy means. Divine Intelligence knows exactly the right way to help my dreams come true.

I get out of the way and let Divine Intelligence work in right action. I let go and let God and it is so.

LESSON NINETEEN

USING INTUITION

While it is true that you are in charge of your own life, it is also true that you can ask for help from a Source greater than your conscious self. We often call this Source intuition. It is an inner connection to God.

You can tune into the God-Center within yourself and get the guidance you need to live your life well. Everyone has intuition at his disposal and everyone can learn to listen within. It may take time to become proficient at the process of inner listening but you can do it.

There are many books and programs which promise to teach you the "secrets of the Universe." Usually, that secret or secrets comes wrapped in fancy language which turns out to say that your thoughts are causing your experiences. This is what Science of Mind teaches as well.

Sometimes people trip themselves up by trying to "figure out" God's will for them. It is as though they view God as a mysterious figure who presents a life puzzle which they must solve.

God's will for you is that you live well and move closer to the knowledge that you and God are one. The form that good life takes is up to you.

You can tune within for guidance and profit from the experience but it is important to be very clear about the nature of that inner guidance which you are getting. You are setting the parameters and direction. Divine Mind will supply answers about how to get there if you ask.

SKILL BUILDERS

1. Sit quietly in a chair and follow your breath until you are quite relaxed. Ask yourself silently, "What can I do to help myself understand my life better?" Sit quietly and let answers (which may come as pictures or words) float in front of your eyes. After a few minutes, open your eyes and write down anything you want.

2. Pick one issue you've been working on for a while, and make a suggestion to yourself before you go to sleep that you will have a dream in which a solution will appear. Keep a note pad by your bed and write down your experience first thing when you wake.

3. Form a regular habit of presenting a creative problem to your intuition and waiting for the answer to surface. Writers do this all the time. For example, you may want to ask your intuition what to do to earn more money. Over the next week, jot down every idea that comes to you.

4. Learn to use free association in your journal keeping. One simple technique is called clustering. Simply write a word that may represent an issue you are working on, such as "diabetes" or "mother" and fill the whole page up with words that freely associate with that word. Later, you may wish to organize the words into categories, steps, statements or affirmations.

AFFIRMATIONS

...I use my intuitive intelligence.
...I listen well to my inner voice.
...I have a powerful ally in my intuition.

TREATMENT

I know that Divine Guidance is available to me at any time. I have only to turn within, become willing to accept revealed truth and listen with an open mind.

Right now, I turn within to that place where I always know a peace which passes understanding. I rest in the knowledge that I am connected to my Source and that I can rely on Divine Guidance whenever I need direction.

I ask for new clarity and direction about:

_____

_____

_____

I release any sense of silliness or sense of doubt. I release any preconceived notions about how to proceed. I release any fear or need to control. I open myself to good.

I am ready to accept good and so it is.

LESSON TWENTY

IT IS ALL ONE

It is all God. It is all One. There is only One Mind.

We completely deny the belief that there is a power for good and another power for evil in the universe. We deny the idea of a Devil. Nor do we believe in original sin. We do not accept any belief in two powers or "duality".

This concept of unity is the platform upon which our whole teaching stands. One cannot believe in "negative powers" or "dark forces" or, "The Devil made me do it," and use the teaching of Science of Mind effectively. One must accept full responsibility and the joy of knowing the power and omnipresence of God.

It is all God and at the level of truth, you and I are never separated from our Source. We are always supported, always loved and always in a position of power.

The old song, "His eye is on the sparrow/ and I know he watches me/" is not the full story. God lives as God *in* the sparrow. The spirit which animates the sparrow's wings and enables it to fly is God. The song the sparrow sings is God's song.

You and I are also animated by the spirit of God. The life we lead is an expression of God's life. Even when we have felt most distant from our Higher Power, we have been as close as our next breath. Even when we are absolutely certain that we have been tempted by the Devil or destroyed by addiction, we have been making our own choices (perhaps based on fear or confusion but from free will).

If we feel we are in bondage to evil, or bound by our past, or damaged by events, we are not yet clear on our relationship to God. We need to rethink our beliefs. We need to stretch our understanding until we truly grasp the concept that we are God in action.

We need to accept our spiritual magnificence!

SKILL BUILDERS

1. Ask yourself if there was ever time when you felt very close to God. (If not, choose a truly happy experience and use it for the following meditation.) Put on some of your favorite music and recapture the memory of that experience, noticing how you feel physically and emotionally. Pay attention to your mood. Notice your breathing. Become aware of your muscle stress. Are you relaxed? Notice as many details as you can. Relive the experience of unification with Source.

2. Find a memory of a time when you felt far from God. See it as though it were a movie in your mind. Now keep that image and begin to bring in the experience of God's closeness from your previous meditation. Reproduce your relaxed breathing while holding the negative picture of yourself. Then let go of the muscular tension. Now notice how your mood is altering. Are you able to keep the image and feel close to Source? Does the image dissolve? Or do you simply see it in a different light?

3. This week, whenever you find yourself judging another person as bad, release that idea and see the person as a spiritual traveler who has temporarily taken a wrong turn. Bless the person and release the action you labeled bad.
4. This week, whenever you feel alone, frightened, worried, concerned, overworked, stressed, sick or tired, reproduce the experience of the first meditation - bring back the emotional and physical experience of closeness to God.

AFFIRMATIONS

...God's life is in the sparrow and I know God's life is in me.
...God is as close to me as my next breath.
...With God, all things are possible and I am with God.

TREATMENT

There is only One Mind, One God, One Creative Intelligence. I am living my life in that One Creative Intelligence. God lives through me and expresses Life through me. I am one with God.

In this moment, I accept full responsibility for my life. I accept that I am creator of my life. I accept that my life is a result of my understanding, my beliefs, my choices, and my acceptance level (up until now).

Now, I change any belief I choose, including _____.
Now, I make new choices, including _____.
Now, I accept the gifts of Spirit, including _____.

I understand my connection to Source. I understand my ability to use the Power of the Universe. I understand my spiritual magnificence.

I let my gratitude overflow as I release this powerful treatment and let spiritual law take care of the details. I let go and I let God.

LESSON TWENTY-ONE

ONE GOD - TWO FUNCTIONS

Although God is only one and we know there is no opposing force - no opposition to the power of God - it sometimes seems as though there are two parts to God. We speak of love and law. We learn about Spirit and Universal Subjectivity. We read about God operating as Spirit through the Universal Medium that we call Soul in Religious Science terminology. We hear about the law of cause and effect. Sometimes we study the action of treatment as Objective Mind and Subjective Mind.

One does not have to understand all the words and charts to use treatment effectively. One does not have to have the logic behind using God Within to do a treatment that will bring changes in our outside circumstances.

Nevertheless, many students of Science of Mind need to have a clearer understanding of how God operates in our individual lives in order to create more effective treatments (and better lives).

Here is a simple explanation for a process you will find more thoroughly explained in the Science of Mind Textbook.

1. There is only One Mind (God or Spirit).
2. That Mind works through us as our thought (Spirit, Conscious Mind, Objective Mind).
3. Our thoughts send messages to a different facet of the One Mind which we call Soul (Subconscious Mind or Subjective Mind).

4. The spiritual law of cause and effect receives the messages and responds by creating a solid version (of the messages) in our lives.

It is important to remember that the two aspects of One Mind are completely different in their functions. Conscious Mind (or Objective Mind or Spirit) has choices. Subconscious Mind (or Subjective Mind or Soul) has the ability to bring things into being but cannot choose. We say that Objective Mind has *volition*. Objective Mind *impregnates* Subjective Mind which must respond because of the spiritual laws of the Universe.

Both aspects of Mind are very powerful. Although Subjective Mind cannot "start" anything, it can find a way to fulfill any demand (which is sometimes called secondary cause) placed on it by Objective Mind.

To repeat, there is One Mind acting in two ways. We have more than one name for the two aspects of the One Mind and all of the explanations and names point to the action of Spirit moving through Soul to become Body. Or, put another way, the process of Objective Mind descending through Subjective Mind to become Form.

All attempts to explain this process of creation are descriptions of our basic belief that Mind comes before Matter or Spirit creates Form.

These ideas, while they may seem complicated, can be traced all the way back to the idealism of the Ancient Greeks. Once you discard the belief that the only things which are real are solid objects which can be weighed and measured, you can easily understand Science of Mind.

SKILL BUILDERS

1. Create a definite message which you wish to send to Subjective Mind. Write that message on several 3 x 5 cards and post the cards around your house. Put one in your wallet. Put one on the dashboard of your car. Place a card on your mirrors, on your refrigerator, on your television set. Each time you read your affirmation, remind yourself that Subjective Mind is your servant.

2. Imagine a sum of money you would like to receive. Create an affirmation for that amount. Now cross the amount out and raise the number. (You may want to double it). As you increase the figure, remind yourself that Subjective Mind has no opinion about the size of the number and must obey the demand made by Objective Mind.

AFFIRMATIONS

...Subjective Mind is my servant.

...I use the law of cause and effect to build a wonderful life.

...I can accept a great deal and I now open my acceptance level to even more.

...Both love and law are supporting my life. I have it all.

TREATMENT

One Mind, One Universal Intelligence.

This One Mind is operating in my life right now as Objective Mind. I am Spirit in action. I am working with Objective Mind to create a new idea for myself. I now accept this new idea which includes _____

_____
_____

_____

This new idea is now released to Subjective Mind which must respond to my clear declaration and definite acceptance. I know that God, functioning as Subjective Mind, is my servant.

I accept this new idea completely and I leave it to Subjective Mind to work out the details. I know that way will open and my work was done when I spoke my word and accepted it. I let go and I let God. And so it is.

LESSON TWENTY-TWO

EVIL DISAPPEARS IN THE LIGHT OF TRUTH

When we begin to study Science of Mind, we soon turn to the issue of evil and we have to let go of some old ideas in order to experience the total benefits of Science of Mind.

You may be accustomed to thinking of the world in terms of good and bad or good and evil but once you understand that God is all there is, you must accept that life can only be good because God is good.

What we are accustomed to calling evil is based on a false idea which we hold about our individual nature or the nature of life. As we move closer to understanding the truth about God being all there is, we stop allowing a belief in evil to control us.

The idea of good and evil is based on the idea of two opposing forces in the world. It is called dualism. Science of Mind teaches unitarianism, not dualism.

The stronger your belief in the unity of God, the stronger your ability to use Science of Mind skills in your life. For example, if you have the experience of an illness and you lie in bed wailing, "Why did this happen to me? Why is God punishing me in this way?" you will have difficulty healing yourself.

However, if you remind yourself of the truth - that God is all there is and that you are connected to God therefore at the level of truth, you are already perfect, whole, healthy, and complete, you will be able to heal very rapidly.

SKILL BUILDERS

1. Make it a point to redirect your thinking whenever you find yourself dwelling on things you consider bad or evil. Remember that what you call evil is brought into existence in the same manner and by the same law as what you call good. You control your experience as you control your thinking.

2. Practice seeing things as whole and complete. If you visit someone in the hospital, make it a point to treat to know that the patient is whole, perfect and complete.

3. Develop the ability to detach yourself from any apparent problem or evil. Consciously put emotional distance between yourself and whatever it is. Know that you do not have to add to the problem by reacting. Be a solution, not a problem.

4. Create a habit of forgiveness. See every person on this planet as a spiritual being on a spiritual journey toward the knowledge of himself as divine. Forgive yourself by knowing there is nothing to forgive. Forgive any other person by knowing there is nothing to forgive.

AFFIRMATIONS

...God is all there is.
...I am one with God.
...There is only unity.
...God is ever present, all powerful, all perfect.
...I attract only good, beauty and joy into my life.

TREATMENT

I know that there is a Power For Good greater than I am in my life and that I am using it now. That Power is called God and it is a unified power. One God. One Mind. One Intelligence.

I now turn to that One God and make a conscious connection. I now recognize that I am never separated and that I can never be separated from my Source. The Universe is for me and there is nothing to fear.

I am at One with God. I am centered in the Truth and the Light. All shadows disappear from my thinking and therefore, from my life. Shadows are simply that - dark spots which have never existed once the lights go on.

I walk in the Light. I am the Light. I dwell in the House of the Lord Forever. Nothing can ever harm or damage me. I am safe. I am in love. I am at peace. I am one with God.

I accept these words as the absolute truth of my being and I allow them to establish a new sense of ease in my life. I let this be so and so it is.

LESSON TWENTY-THREE

CHOOSING POSITIVE EXPERIENCES

Many people feel as though they have no control over their lives at all. They see life as filled with unexplained, chaotic events which may upset them at any moment. These people usually view death as the ultimate evil but will cite a long list of other reasons to suffer. The reasons may include anything from a dread disease to not being accepted to a particular college.

You can observe that the more people feel as though they are victims of outside events, the more unhappy and unsuccessful they are. This is one of the ways in which you can begin to "prove" Science of Mind to yourself.

People who believe they have little or no control over their lives are correct. They are letting life control them. They are recreating negative patterns without consciously choosing them.

It is also true that people who believe they are in charge of their own destinies do have a wonderful impact on the direction their lives take. You can also observe this characteristic in your associates, friends and family.

Your life right now is a result of conscious and unconscious choices you have made. If that is difficult for you to believe, don't turn away from Science of Mind entirely. Use this modified statement and observe life closely. Your life right now is *primarily* a result of conscious and unconscious choices you have made.

The more conscious you are about what you are choosing to think and do, the greater your ability to control your life. Much of what you have called evil or bad can be avoided in the future. For example, if someone is in a "bad" relationship with an "evil" man and she believes it is because fate led her to marry the wrong person, she will be unhappy. If that same person comes to realize she made an unconscious decision to repeat failure patterns and that she is free to change those patterns now, she can quickly find a way to happiness. Her way to happiness can take myriad forms but it must begin with taking responsibility for changing her own belief system.

If this person relies on "luck" to change her "fate" and the "evil" man leaves her, she will find another difficult partner and start the pattern over again. The next guy may take a new way of expressing negativity but her unhappiness will find a way to recreate itself unless something breaks the pattern of negative thinking.

SKILL BUILDERS

1. Do you see any negative patterns operating in your life now?
2. Do you see any negative patterns which may have operated in your life when you were younger?
3. Select one pattern and ask yourself what belief needs to be changed before the pattern is erased. Is there more than one belief involved?
4. Write an affirmation you can begin to believe in order to begin to dislodge this pattern.

AFFIRMATIONS

...*I am creating a wonderful life for myself right now.*

...*I deserve the best and I create the best.*

...*I am a positive thinker.*

...*I love myself and I take good care of my mental outlook.*

TREATMENT

I recognize that there is a Creative Power operating in my life right now. This Power is fulfilling directions which I give as I become more and more conscious about how I live my life. I do have choices and those choices include wonderful opportunities to live life more abundantly.

I choose to live my life successfully and well. I rely on Divine Intelligence to supply the necessary solutions to any apparent problems. I choose the very best for myself. I choose to be happy, to be loving and to be wealthy.

These choices of mine are conscious, powerful and directed choices. I identify with the very best and I allow those situations, people, and things which I admire to be in my life. All negative situations and problems simply fall away as I move more and more into the realm of positive choices.

I choose the best. I choose health. I choose wealth. I choose joy. I choose fun. I choose love. I choose creativity. I choose to know the truth which sets me free. I choose to expand my horizons, extend my vision and live life abundantly right here and now.

Having made these positive choices, I am now ready to turn it over to God. I allow Divine Intelligence to shape and implement my new choices. I accept wonderful results and so it is.

LESSON TWENTY-FOUR

YOU ALWAYS HAVE A CHOICE

Much of what we label evil or negative is simply our emotional response to something which we can change in our lives as we take control of our thinking.

Other things which we call bad may be best changed by eliminating a negative emotional response. It may be true that there are certain situations, conditions, or experiences in our lives which are less than optimal. Some of these may take a long time to change or it is even possible that they may not change at all.

If you are a mature person and are only five feet tall, it is probably good to work on accepting your height rather than trying to grow another six inches. If you are over fifty and wanted to be a ballet dancer, it is probably a good idea to look for another creative outlet instead of feeling miserable about a perceived limitation.

There is an art to knowing what you can and cannot change and the Serenity Prayer can be very helpful. *God grant me the serenity to accept the things I cannot change, the courage to change the things I can, and the wisdom to know the difference.*

One thing that you can always change is your attitude. You always have a choice about how to feel about any experience. This does not mean you should just "grin and bear it". But it does mean you should take a realistic look at your emotional responses to life's challenges.

One person can stay home from a party because of a broken fingernail. Another person can run a race while in a wheelchair. You can always choose to be happy right now.

SKILL BUILDERS

1. Make a list of anything you believe needs to be fixed before you can be happy.
2. Separate the things you can change from the things another person must change. For example, if you think you must lose 10 pounds to be happy, put it in list A. If you think Uncle Charlie must stop drinking in order for you to be happy, put that in list B.
3. Rewrite the items you have control over as affirmations.
   For example, write an affirmation such as, "I am at my perfect weight now."
4. Make yourself a promise not to think about the items on list B for a while. Give Uncle Charlie a rest. He will stop drinking when he wants. In the meantime, you have a right to be happy.
5. Remember the best time you can remember when you were happy. Now use your imagination to recapture the feeling (not the situation). During the day, conjure up that feeling and let yourself feel happy.
6. Ask yourself if you really believe you have to fix everything before you can be happy. Keep asking yourself that question every time you are tempted to get tangled up in unhappiness over something you cannot control.
7. This day, every time something comes up which might throw you off balance, remind yourself, "I have a choice about how I feel about this."

8. Practice smiling at everyone you meet. Even if it feels silly, do it. If you can manage to be brave enough, say hello to a couple of respectable strangers.
9. Try watching only happy movies and reading happy books for a month. Keep a record and see if there are any noticeable changes in your happiness level.
10. Refuse to rehash tragic situations with friends. If it is a new issue, be courteous. If it is the same old soap opera, change the subject. Keep bringing the conversation around to something cheerful. If that is a problem for you or your friend, try looking at that. What does it mean in terms of your personal goals?

AFFIRMATIONS

...I am a happy person.
...I am happy right now, in this place, with this person.
...I am choosing to react with joy to this event.
...I choose my reactions to every event.
...Only joy comes to me. I am joy personified.
...My smile signals joy, attracting happiness to me.
...My laughter rings like a bell, singing joy and bringing joy to me.

TREATMENT

I am in tune with an Infinite Intelligence which surrounds me, supports me and supplies my every need. I allow myself to relax and depend on the Infinite Intelligence to supply my every need.

Right now, I am guided by Infinite Intelligence to raise the quality of my life tremendously. I accept more of every good than I ever have before.

Infinite Intelligence helps me set new directions where needed and it helps me to see my current situation with new eyes. I am in tune with the Universe. I am at One with the Universe. I choose to be happy, healthy, wealthy and wise and the Universe supplies the way. And so it is.

LESSON TWENTY-FIVE

POSITIVE PROOF

The Science of Mind textbook begins with this phrase, "*We all look forward to the day when science and religion shall walk hand in hand through the visible to the invisible.*" One of the things this means is that everything we teach in Science of Mind can be proven by observing that the principles actually work.

We use the word demonstrate to mean proof. For example, we can treat for money and when we get money, we are said to have "demonstrated" money but what we have really demonstrated is that treatment works.

Our basic teaching is that form follows thought. Therefore, one can also work backwards, by looking at what is going on in life and knowing that a thought is behind it. For example, if I am experiencing a series of unhappy love affairs, I can assume that there is something in my thought patterns about love that needs to be healed.

The easiest way to understand the concept of demonstration is to think of the old saying, "The proof is in the pudding." That means you are using the correct recipe if the pudding tastes good and doesn't seem flat. You can also assume that you are using the correct thoughts if you life tastes good and doesn't seem flat.

You can also assume that you should change your thoughts if there is something in the "taste of your pudding" that you'd like to change.

SKILL BUILDERS

1. What am I demonstrating in my life today? Make a list.
2. Divide the items on the list into that which you wish to keep and that which you wish to discard. For example, put kindness in list A and put poverty in list B.
3. Rephrase everything in list A into affirmations. For example, "I am kindness and love."
4. Change everything in list B into an opposite affirmation. For example, "I am rich."
5. Remembering that praise attracts more of the same, make it a point to speak praise out loud for each of the items on list A. For example, find a way to say out loud, "I have always been a kind person and I am glad that is so."
6. Whenever you have an honest opportunity to praise yourself for something on list B, do so. For example, "I think I am really making progress on my wealth goals. I've saved $10.00 this week."
7. As you speak your praise out loud, notice the response of the people who are listening. You may want to be more selective and spend more time with people who support you in your spiritual work. You may choose to talk less or about other things with people who cannot find a way to be supportive. You have that right.
8. Watch that you don't speak in negative ways about yourself. If you slip and say something like, "I am bad with money," erase it orally as well as mentally. Immediately follow up with "I am really making strides in my money sense." Other people aren't the only ones who believe what you tell

them about yourself. Your subconscious also believes it. Divine Mind has no opinion about how much money you should have and will simply respond to whatever you say. Say you want the best for yourself. Say it often. Say it clearly. Say it decisively. Say it with a smile and happy expectation.

9. Keep a scientific record of your results. Date your entries and make specific notes. You will build your effectiveness as you build the strength of your beliefs. Observing results is the way to prove Science of Mind works. This is not a system which requires faith. The science part means you can prove it.

AFFIRMATIONS

...My life is sweet.
...My life is has plenty of spice in it.
...My life is rich.
...My life is healthy.
...My life is love.
...I love life.
...Life loves me.
...I am willing to change whatever needs changing.
...I am grateful for the wonderful demonstrations in my life.

TREATMENT

My life is linked to an unlimited Power for Good. My life is linked with Eternal Life. My life is linked with Truth, Beauty, Joy, Wisdom, Riches, Love and Health.

Right now, I allow more of the gifts of Spirit to enter my life than I have ever been able to accept before. I allow my acceptance level to rise, to widen and to open to Unlimited Good. I am willing to receive and give. I am willing to be in the flow of life. I am willing to open up and live at a totally new level of existence. I am willing to change whatever needs to change. I am willing to let go of whatever needs to be released. I am willing to stretch and grow and prosper and change.

I let this treatment go, knowing that it is a seed planted in the mind of God and that it flowers in wonderful abundant ways in my life now. And so it is.

LESSON TWENTY-SIX

HEALTHY RELATIONSHIPS

Many people are convinced that someone else needs to change before they can be happy. For instance, a woman who has been in a marriage with an abusive husband will often come for counseling and talk all hour about how "he" needs to change.

Science of Mind teaches us to mind our own business. This is a concept which comes easily for some and takes practice for others. Remember, as we mind our own business, we grow stronger and braver and all our relationships will change.

For example, the woman in the bad marriage who studies Science of Mind any time at all will find that change comes in one form or another. However, change can only happen if we work on ourselves.

There is no one answer to any problem and there is more than one way change can take place. Either she will stop responding to her husband in a way that holds patterns into place and he will go find someone else to play games with or he will change without direct interference. Or she may quickly grow to love herself enough that she leaves the relationship. Once out, her spiritual work will make it certain that she no longer attracts this sort of person.

The important point in any relationship work is to understand that all change is within ourselves. We do not use Science of Mind "on" someone else. We use it on ourselves. Nevertheless, serious spiritual work, will surely lead to better responses from others and better relationships.

SKILL BUILDERS

1. Choose one person who you would like to feel better about. Draw a mental circle of God's love and put yourself in the center. Now imagine that person is also inside the circle. You do not need to do anything or say anything. Just see yourself inside the same wonderful circle of love.
2. Think of your current relationships and see if there is a pattern you wish to change. Write it down.
3. Visualize those relationships without the pattern. For example, if you have several friends who do nothing but complain about their husbands when you see them, visualize yourselves laughing and talking about something else.
4. Are you in a sexual relationship with one person at the moment? Is that relationship an expression of love? How would you need to change to have that relationship be more loving? (Do not fall into the trap of thinking how he/she needs to change).
5. Would you like to be in a sexual relationship with someone at this time? Do you see any obstacles? Write them down. For example, you may be holding a belief such as, "Smart women are only interested in careers - they don't want to marry anymore." or "There are no available men left in the world!"
6. Take a look at the beliefs you are holding which seem to be obstacles. Begin to heal the beliefs. This is where to begin work.

AFFIRMATIONS

...I am loveable.

...I am attracting the right person into my life now.

...I am in only loving relationships.

...All my relationships are a reflection of that which is best in my thinking.

TREATMENT

I know that God is Love and Love is God in action. I also know that I live, move and have my being in God. Therefore, I must be Love in action.

I also know that I must reflect in order to experience that which I desire. I now choose to reflect love. I declare that I am love in action, right here and now.

I am in loving relationship with the Universe and everyone in this life. I am especially in loving relationship with _____.

I choose to be love. I choose to reflect love. I choose to attract love. I choose to understand love in new and wonderful ways.

I let this treatment go, knowing that it is taking root in the Mind of God and that it flowers and blooms in my life now.

LESSON TWENTY-SEVEN

YOU ARE NOT A VICTIM

When we know that we are creating our own experience, we take charge of our lives in new and wonderful ways. We no longer feel or behave like victims. We no longer need to fear others.

Two things are operating here. We are changing our mental atmosphere by changing our thinking, therefore bringing more positive experiences into our lives. Also, we are no longer reacting to other people's actions but we are acting out of our own center of truth.

For example, if you have a boss at work who always picks on you and you begin to really employ Science of Mind to alter your thinking about this issue, you will see great change. Some of that change may come through your altered self esteem - you may demand better treatment and get it or you may behave in a way that makes the boss more comfortable and relaxed so that he no longer feels a need to pick on you.

Some of the change may come because you no longer let anyone else control your emotions. No matter what your boss says, you can refuse to feel bad about yourself. For this reason, it is never correct to say, "You hurt my feelings". No one can ever hurt your feelings because you always have a choice in the way you respond.

SKILL BUILDERS

1. Imagine yourself sitting in a chair beside the telephone and hearing it ring. You have a choice whether or not to pick it up. Choose not to respond. Feel the power in that choice.

2. Next time someone says something to you that you would have considered threatening or painful, remind yourself that you can choose not to respond. Say to yourself, "I have the power to decide whether to let this bother me or not." Notice your reaction and make a note of it in your journal.

3. Imagine yourself with someone who often says or does things you consider troubling. Imagine that person pulling one of his tricks. Imagine yourself not responding. Feel the power in that choice.

4. See yourself surrounded by a ball of white light. See that ball as being an invisible shield which no one or no thing can penetrate unless you permit it. Feel the loving protection and claim it as your own.

AFFIRMATIONS

...*I am always protected and surrounded by God's love.*
...*I choose how I respond to people and events. I have the power.*
...*I am centered in peace.*
...*I am a beacon of light and strength even in turbulent waters.*
...*I attract wonderful people into my life.*
...*I am a center of poise, strength and courage.*

TREATMENT

I rejoice in life, knowing that Universal Intelligence is operating at all times, places, and in all people. I do not need to straighten anyone out. I do not need to make anyone love me. I am at home in the life of God and I am perfectly independent and happy to be alive.

I don't need anyone to validate my existence. I exist and I am enough. I am life everlasting. I don't depend on anyone else to make me feel good about myself. I am already bursting with love for myself and that spills out into love for others. I am love knowing itself as love.

I let go of all fear. I let go of all need to please others. I let go of all shyness. I let go of all shame. I let go of all sense of rejection or anger. I let go of all nonsense so that I can experience the love that is mine by right of Divine Inheritance.

The right people are drawn to me and everyone who is in my orbit sees me as love. I see them as love as well. All is good and so it is.

LESSON TWENTY-EIGHT

BEGIN WITH SELF LOVE

Learning to love yourself is the key to establishing healthy relationships with others. You simply cannot expect anyone else to love you enough to fill up the empty places in your heart. Love is primarily an inside job.

Many of us spend a great deal of time and energy looking for someone to love us enough so that we can love ourselves. Many of us have hungered for a secure sense of being loved ever since we were small children.

It is painful to feel unloved and we must find a way to break old patterns of belief about ourselves if we want to feel happiness. Those negative belief patterns often revolve around believing we are unlovable.

Since we are all created in the image and likeness of God, we must all be loveable. While it is true that we may have done things in our life we choose not to repeat, it can never be true that we have been permanently damaged or hurt by those earlier experiences. We are unlimited life. We always were and always will be whole, perfect and complete.

Learning to love oneself usually depends on contacting that whole, perfect and complete truth which lives within each of us. As we begin to accept ourselves in a loving manner, we begin to give off a different message to the world and others react more favorably as well.

If you would be loved - if you would be loving - you must first learn to love yourself. That is spiritual law in operation.

SKILL BUILDERS

1. Each day for a week, stand in front of the mirror and look deep into your own eyes. Say, "I love you very much. I love you exactly as you are right here and now. You are wonderful."
2. Make an never ending list of the things you like about yourself. Include the big ideas and also include some smaller ones such as , "I love the way my hair curls when it rains." Be silly - fall in love with yourself. It's fun!
3. Monitor your speech for a day. Notice whether you make negative comments or jokes about yourself. If so, correct yourself immediately, replacing the slur with a complement. You need to speak only praise.

AFFIRMATIONS

...I am a wonderful person.

...Someone is/will be very lucky to love me.

...I love myself just the way I am.

...I am perfect, whole and complete.

...I love myself as is.

TREATMENT

I recognize that Universal Intelligence made me in its own image and that I live, move and have my being in that Universal Intelligence. There could be no mistake when I was born. I am not a mistake. I am a wonderful, cooperative, living enterprise of God's. God knows itself through me. I am important. I am wonderful and I am love itself.

Since I am permanently and definitely connected to my Source, I cannot need anything. I cannot want. I cannot suffer. I cannot be lonely, ashamed or sad. I am life knowing itself as life and I rejoice in that knowledge. I am glad to be alive.

I love life. I love myself. I love others. I know the truth which sets me free. I am connected to others through the Source and I am whole perfect and complete. I am made of the same stuff as God itself and I am wonderful.

I rely upon Universal Intelligence to know me as I know it. All is well.

LESSON TWENTY-NINE

ABUNDANT LIFE

One of the most prevalent false ideas in our society is that there isn't enough to go around. Once we understand that Spirit provides whatever we can accept, we can begin to let go of the idea of scarcity.

The very nature of God is abundance. Jesus taught this in the story of the loaves and fishes. We can see the way good things multiply in our lives as we become tuned in to spiritual ideas.

Understanding that there is enough to go around changes the way we look at everything. It frees us to be ourselves and it frees others to be themselves.

SKILL BUILDERS

1. Consider the lilies of the fields. Make a list of everything in the world you can think of that comes in multitudes. Begin with the stars and move on to drops of water and cells in your body.
2. Keep this list going all week. Add to it until you really see the pattern of abundance which pervades the universe.

AFFIRMATIONS

...*There is plenty to go around.*

...*Abundant living is my Divine Inheritance.*

...*I have as many ideas as there are stars in the skies.*

...*I have as much money as there is water in the ocean.*

...*I have as much love as there is sand on the beaches of the world.*

...*I have as much health as there are grasses in the plains of the world.*

TREATMENT

Universal Intelligence is the basis of this life of mine and I am an integral part of that unlimited intelligence. I am at one with my Source and that Source is unlimited.

I am unlimited in my ability to express abundance in my life. I accept more each day and my prosperity multiplies like the grains of sand on the beach, the waves in the ocean and the leaves of grass. My life is God's life and I can never want for anything. I am tuned into my Infinite Source and so it is.

LESSON THIRTY

MONEY AND SPIRIT

Money matters are spiritual matters. Your thoughts are constantly directing the Universe to produce new experiences. As you change your thinking, your experiences will change. This works on the psychological level and it also works on what people call the "material" level. Today, you are going to practice wealth building at the thought level.

SKILL BUILDERS

1. Spend ten or fifteen minutes imagining what your world will be like when all your money issues are dissolved. Will you still be working at your current job? To whom will you give gifts? What will you look like? What will you wear? How and where will you live? Jot down ideas on a piece of paper. If critical thoughts about the exercise come up, remind yourself that it is a skill building lesson and you are being a good student. Stay out of judgment or criticism of yourself.

2. If the first exercise was difficult for you, resolve to repeat it every day for a week. Then repeat it one time a week until you have internalized the vision of your wealthy self. The more you can begin to feel wealthy, the easier it will be for money to come to you.

3. Make it a project to make a list of all you will do when money no longer is an issue. Pay attention to your desires. They are clues to growth and change.

4. There are two simple approaches to solving money problems, earn more or spend less. Notice your reaction to that statement. Do you have emotional responses such as, "*I don't waste any money now.*" or "*I'm already working very hard.*" Jot down your negative feelings about your relationship to money. This is the place to begin the healing work.

5. Take any negative statements you have written and rewrite them as affirmations. Some examples follow:

"*I don't have time to get a second job.*" becomes "*I have plenty of time and money.*"

"*I want to be more spiritual, I'm not interested in money.*" becomes "*Money is one expression of God in action.*"

"*I've always been poor with money.*" becomes "*I am good with money, right now.*"

AFFIRMATIONS

...*Money loves me and I love money.*

...*Money is God in action.*

...*Money is my friend.*

...*I choose money and I use money.*

...*Money is one expression of Creative Energy.*

...*I am a money magnet.*

TREATMENT

I know that Divine Intelligence operates in every aspect of life and that there is no such thing as separation of spirit and matter. All material blessings come from spirit and are available as we are able to receive them.

I know that I am living my life as God's expression of itself and that I am able to express what I can accept. I choose to accept and express more of life's blessings this day than I ever have before. I choose to be rich.

I let go of any outmoded ideas about separation of money and God. I let go of any outmoded ideas about money or the love of money being evil. There is no evil. There is only love.

I release anything in my past which may have stood in the way of my expressing a fully rich life up to this point. I release all known or unknown beliefs which have stood in the way of demonstrating wealth as a part of my truth.

I open my mind. I open my heart. I open my eyes and ears. I accept wealth as a part of my divine inheritance. I accept guidance as to the steps I can take to acquire wealth. I am willing to be guided and I am willing to have riches now. I am a willing co-creator of my Universe.

Life is a banquet and I am hungry for life. I join the feast, taking my rightful place and filling my life with material plenty. I let this treatment do its work, knowing that it is done in the mind of God and so it is.

LESSON THIRTY-ONE

ATTRACTING MONEY

Attracting money into our lives can be quite simple once we understand that what we praise and pay attention to will come to us.

It is useless to treat for more money if you harbor the belief that money is evil or that people who have money are not nice people. Watch what you say about money and be sure to praise it when you speak of it. Never use words such as "filthy lucre" or expressions such as "filthy rich", even in jest.

SKILL BUILDERS

1. When you pay your bills, say, "I thank God for the abundance which is mine", each time you write a check.
2. When you give money to charity or to your church or to a friend, say, "This money returns to me multiplied."
3. Visualize money as very light. See dollar bills blowing around in the air. Now see them blowing in through your window and landing on your lap. Put a lot of them in your pocket. Enjoy the feeling of having so much money surrounding you that it is foolish to try and hold onto it.
4. Visualize money as fluid and liquid. Imagine money as being water running over glistening rocks. See money running over a waterfall. See liquid money falling into a huge lake. Claim the lake and know that whenever you want money you can dip down and pull it up.

5. Get quiet and listen to see if you have any old painful thoughts surrounding money. Write them down and begin to heal the areas of hurt. You may find shame or anger or other old tapes. Know that you can heal any belief easily by allowing yourself to love yourself. You are not your past. You are God in action. Money is God in action. You are money. Money is you.

6. Begin to pay attention to money on a day to day basis. Read the financial pages in your magazines and newspapers. Tune into the financial news on t.v. Take a course in budgeting or financial planning. Increase your skills level as a step toward attracting more money. Remember that we get what we focus on. Too many people say they want money and never learn anything about it at all.

7. Keep a money journal. Jot down any ideas you have about getting or keeping money and consider following through with them. Once you decide to acquire more money, Divine Intelligence will offer suggestions.

AFFIRMATIONS
...There is enough to go around.
...I am rich now.
...I am now rich.
...I live a prosperous life.
...My life is abundance personified.

TREATMENT

God is everywhere, spilling out abundance because abundance is the nature of God. As there are hundreds of billions of grains of sand and hundreds of billions of leaves of grass, there are hundreds of billions of ideas which bring me happiness.

I accept happiness as a part of the abundance of the Universe. I accept riches as a part of that happiness. I accept a life of peace and plenty as a part of the Divine Plan.

I am ready to accept a great deal of wealth and a great deal of happiness. I know that there is enough to go around and that I am entitled to enjoy the very best that life has to offer. I am glad to be alive and my gladness manifests as financial freedom.

As there are fish in the sea, birds in the sky, sand on the beaches, flowers in the fields, there are dollars in my pockets. I can never be without because I am a part of this abundant Universe. And so it is!

LESSON THIRTY-TWO

MONEY, MONEY, MONEY

Many of us have a lot of resistance to letting money flow freely into our lives. We put up barriers which take myriad forms. We spend too much or save too much or even give away too much. We invest it foolishly in get rich quick schemes or we simply let it dribble away at the malls.

There are almost as many reasons why people block the flow of money as there are people so it is not fruitful to spend a lot of time searching out the psychological reasons for poverty. Far better to spend one's time in visualization and treatment activities.

You can overcome a belief or behavior without ever knowing what it is or why it is if you are willing. Become willing to be rich!

SKILL BUILDERS

1. Notice the people around you and see how many handle money foolishly.
2. Ask yourself if you have ever been foolish about money.
3. Ask yourself if you would like to change any of your current money behaviors.
4. Set some realistic goals for this week.
5. Set some realistic goals for this month.
6. Set some realistic goals for this year.

7. If you continue to follow your realistic goals for five years, where might you be? Imagine the effect of consistent planning and follow through.
8. Prepare a treasure map (collage from magazine) depicting the possible success of the next five years if you follow through on your goals.

AFFIRMATIONS

...I am in charge of my life.
...I am in charge of my spending.
...Money is a favorite friend of mine.
...I handle money well.
...I am good with money.
...I am an excellent investor.

TREATMENT

Money is fluid and it now flows into my life in great quantities. I stop blocking the flow and allow God to pour riches into my life. I do not resist my good.

I decide to drop all psychological money issues this day and open myself up to God's blessings. I allow myself to rely on God as my Source and not to stop the flow. I give up fear, resentment, worry, doubt, guilt, shame, nonsense and I just let it flow.

Money comes to me from many sources and I accept it gracefully and easily.

Money flows in from a great many tributaries, creating a wide and deep river of supply. I dip into the reservoir of liquid money without fear, knowing that money is an idea of God and that God is always in action.

I live, move and have my being as prosperity. Prosperity includes a lot of money. It includes a beautiful home, time to enjoy life, wonderful friends, marvelous possessions, good transportation, excellent recreation and freedom to be and do what I want to do.

I am no longer bound by fear or limitation. I am conscious of my expansive nature and I am totally deaf to that "mothervoice" that says watch out or you'll fail. I know I am a success, live as a success and I rejoice that this is so. And so it is.

I accept success. I accept money. I accept love. I accept greatness. I accept recognition. I accept joy. I accept freedom. I know and fully accept that there is enough to go around and that I have earned mine by right of consciousness which I have developed through my Science of Mind training.

I let this treatment go into the Mind of God where it forms, shapes, and creates wonderful financial circumstances in my life immediately. I know that the work is done because I have accepted this treatment wholeheartedly. I let this be so and so it is.

LESSON THIRTY-THREE

PAYING THE PRICE

You can have anything if you are willing to pay the mental and spiritual coin necessary to get it. In other words, you must be willing to work at this teaching to reap its full benefits.

Science of Mind does not teach wishful thinking techniques. It teaches that you can take charge of your thoughts and gradually come to have control over every aspect of your experience.

You can have a great deal of wealth and financial success if you are willing to take the steps which are necessary to achieve it. Those steps include establishing a vision and really achieving an emotional acceptance of that vision.

In order to achieve a greater level of acceptance, it is often necessary to eradicate false beliefs. Sometimes this can be painful. Often, people must establish a new and richer sense of self worth before they achieve true financial prosperity.

Sometimes people who have issues which center around prosperity are given to magical thinking or "get rich quick" schemes. They would rather buy lottery tickets and hope for the best than pay the mental and spiritual coin of finding lucrative work and saving their money.

Some of our most troublesome thinking mistakes become apparent in prosperity work. Few of us would insist on eating chocolate eclairs and lying on the couch all day as a path to physical well being. Yet more of us want to find our way to financial health without changing any of our work or spending habits.

Before you treat for a million dollars and expect it to fall out of the sky, ask yourself if you've learned to spend less than you make. You need to establish different saving and spending patterns before any amount of money will do the trick.

When you make a financial plan that you believe will work and follow through with it you will surely achieve success. Make sure your plan seems sensible to you. Do not plan to win a million dollars on the lottery by buying 10 tickets a week because you will have too much trouble believing in your plan at a subconscious level.

Before you make your plan, list goals which seem realistic and tailor your financial plan to those goals. For example, if you establish a goal of being debt free by the end of the year, your plan may include a decision to treat for this on a daily basis. It might also include a plan to put 10% of everything you earn into a spiritual tithe or you might plan to save 10% of everything you earn and 100% of any "unexpected" money into above minimum payoff on your credit cards. You can be debt free very quickly if you follow such a plan.

Perhaps you are already quite solvent and you've discovered that you want to retire early in order to start a new career as a painter. Your plan might include selling the Mercedes and buying a Ford to start your early retirement account. You might consult a reputable broker and begin an aggressive stock buying program. You and your broker might decide to concentrate on small blue chip companies which are likely to grow at a better than average rate. By treating daily and cutting out the "extras" and adding all "unexpected" income to your account, you will be painting full time very quickly.

Please note that your financial plans should be practical and they are supported by daily treatment work. Do not believe that you can go against the conservative advice of experts and "trust in the Lord" to make a killing in the commodities market. Unless you are highly skilled, keep your financial plans conservative. Do not turn all your money over to someone who says he is a spiritual advisor to invest for you.

Part of becoming conscious about money is to see how it is confused with other issues in your mind. Some people confuse love with money. While it is true that everything comes from One Source, it is also true that love and money are quite different. Love is a feeling exchanged without price of expectation of payment. Money is a symbol we use for exchanging material objects such as food, clothing and housing.

Spend some time looking at your current life issues and separate them into love, money, health and creativity columns. While it is true that all issues can be resolved through self love and spiritual understanding, it is often helpful to figure out whether you are really staying in that difficult relationship because you hope for love or are afraid to lose the money.

I believe that a clear understanding of Science of Mind principles will result in an abundance of money. Do not make the mistake of believing you are "too spiritual" to have enough money. If you are truly understanding this book, you will notice an increase in your financial abundance.

Consider the possibility of measuring your spiritual understanding and growth by how much money you have. I am not saying that people who have more money are more spiritual. I am only suggesting that your bank balance might be a way for you to measure your individual progress. If you now have a net worth of $15,000 and you really begin to understand and apply your Science of Mind skills, you will have a net worth of $150,000 quickly. Money is the easiest way place to demonstrate principle for many people.

SKILL BUILDERS

1. Go back and read this lesson again. Notice when and if you don't agree with what is written. Ask yourself what you do believe and write it down. Does it make sense in terms of your other learning or is it based on old notions?
2. Make a list of financial goals you believe you can achieve this year.
3. Make a plan which is a blueprint for achieving them. Make sure you include spiritual work. There is nothing any more practical than doing a treatment. However, you will probably speed up the process of increasing your prosperity if you also work and control your spending.

AFFIRMATIONS

...I am a wealthy woman/man.
...Riches love me and I love riches.
...Unlimited treasure surrounds me and supports my every endeavor.

TREATMENT

I understand that the Gifts of Spirit are mine for the envisioning and accepting. I now accept more financial prosperity than ever before. I see life as a banquet laden with treasure and I choose to have a great deal of life's riches.

I attract wealth easily and quickly. This wealth comes to me in the form of money, art, investments, real estate and collections. I am a money magnet. I am surrounded by the loveliest and the best and that is perfectly natural for me.

My expectations are high and they are met. Money flows into my life as though it were water running downhill. I understand that money is fluid, and that all obstacles to an abundant life are now washed away.

I am joyful about my finances. My abundance is apparent and well deserved. I deserve the best and I enjoy the best and so it is.

LESSON THIRTY-FOUR

RAGS TO RICHES

You are always in a transformational mode. You are always changing, growing and evolving into someone new, different and wonderful. You are never stuck.

As a beginning writing student, I was taught that every story is a variation of the Cinderella theme and as a minister, I have learned that there is undiscovered promise in each of us.

Writers know that the main character must be transformed in order to have a story. As humans, we sense that the true plots of our lives circle around transcendence and transformation. No matter how ordinary we look to others, we know the truth. Our lives are rich with promise and pregnant with dreams. We are all Cinderella.

At a very central level, we know ourselves as fledgling butterflies. We dream of achieving great riches, great honors and great love. I believe our dreams persist because they are based on spiritual truths which can not be denied.

There are more variations of Cinderella than any other Western folk tale because transformation is so central to our lives. The ability to change and grow is the basis of all religions. Our lives are spiritual journeys of transformation.

Even the most casual movie-goer must notice that most stories are transformational journeys. *Pretty Woman* was a modern version of Cinderella but for that matter, so was *Dances with Wolves*. So were *Roman Holiday*, *Gypsy*, *Regarding Henry*, and *Fried Green Tomatoes*.

Recently, Bill Moyers hosted an hour long PBS special about the 17th century English spiritual *Amazing Grace*. The song was written by an ex slaver who reformed and went on to become a minister. Moyers marvelled at the popularity of the song among black and white church congregations as well as popular singers. He presented the numerous variations as an intriguing mystery. As I watched and enjoyed the show, I found no mystery behind the enduring popularity of the hymn. It is a celebration of spiritual transformation which resonates truth.

We are capable of changing for the better no matter what we have done in the past and no matter what has been done to us. As we change, we move from that poor little bag of bones who sits by the hearth and feels sorry for herself, into the wonderful princess who sparkles in the glass slippers.

The first step in transformation is the decision to change. Once you have a vision of the direction you would like to go, begin to see yourself as already having arrived. Stop huddling in the cinders and feeling sorry for yourself. You are not trapped. Step out and join the dance of life. Start sparkling and begin to change your thinking.

Transformation is an inside job and waiting for Prince Charming is a waste of time. You are not only your own Cinderella, you are also Prince Charming (capable of action) and your own Fairy Godmother (your mind has the power).

Taking charge of you own transformation is easy when you feel connected to your God Source. You do not have to do the job alone, you can rely on

Universal Spirit to provide the means once you have made your decision and visualized your results. God wants you to succeed. You were put on this earth to express life abundantly.

SKILL BUILDERS
1. Look back five, ten and fifteen years and make a list of the positive life changes you have accomplished.
2. Make a list of things you would like to change in the future. Circle the ones you can begin to work on now.

AFFIRMATIONS
...I am a butterfly.
...I am a beautiful butterfly.
...My life is full of wonderful promise.

TREATMENT
I acknowledge that my life is connected to a larger life which is always changing, always in flux and which is Life Itself. I live, move and have my being in Eternal Life.

I also acknowledge that my life is spiraling upward with the general nature of God and that my particular life is a flexible, positive, loving adventure. I am a beautiful butterfly, emerging with a gorgeous new set of wings this day. I am

Cinderella, moving from an experience of poverty into recognition of my true nature of royalty and opulence. I am a phoenix, rising from ashes and flying free. I am beautiful, free and soaring to new heights. And so it is.

LESSON THIRTY-FIVE

RIGHT WORK

I believe the happiest people in the world are the ones who love their work. We spend so much of our time at work that it is truly unfortunate when we don't enjoy it.

It's one thing not to like hockey games or dentist appointments but it's a much bigger thing not to like your job. No matter how bad your teeth are, the dentist office is a small part of your life.

Work takes up eight or more hours of your life, five days a week, fifty weeks a year. The average worker who goes to his job and/or jobs for forty years totals 80,000 hours before overtime.

Science of Mind teaches you can change your life by changing your thinking and the workplace is an excellent place to begin practicing mental change.

Suppose you had a job you hated and didn't want to leave? What could you do? If you daily practiced telling yourself you love your work and you acted as if you did love your work, you would see some remarkable results very quickly. Imagine for a moment, putting your heart into what you are doing for a month. Imagine you were as enthusiastic about your work as you are about the Saturday afternoon shopping sprees or football games. What would the results be?

If you change your thinking, you are changing your mental atmosphere - the message you are sending to the Universe. The Universe will begin to respond in new ways because it is bound by spiritual laws. Quite simply, if you send out a message of unhappiness, the Universe will provide more unhappiness.

Begin to send out a message of happiness and the Universe will return more happiness. Start your day declaring that you love your work and watch the Universe unfold in love.

The first thing that might happen is that your co-workers would begin to see you in a new way and their attitudes would also change. Just as misery is contagious, so is a positive attitude. Your mental work might change the whole atmosphere where you earn your money.

Another result of your changed attitude might be that your days seem shorter and more interesting and you actually do begin to love your work. However, the chances are very good that you would receive an advancement or some new opportunity would come along before you formed a permanent attachment to that job you used to hate.

Many people recoil when they hear suggestions like "act as if you love your work" or "tell yourself you love your work". They recoil because they believe that if they get too comfortable in the current position they will never be able to make the change. That is simply not true. Loving your work creates opportunities to move ahead. Hating your work digs a cycle of despair much deeper than before.

Consider ten young people who have jobs as baggers in a grocery store. When an opening as a clerk comes up, the manager isn't going to say, "We'll keep Timmy as a bagger because he loves it and promote Lisa to checker because she hates her work." My grandmother used to say, "Cream rises to the top." That was in the old days before pasteurized, defatted milk. Good cooks used cream in those days and they counted on the physical laws which always worked. They skimmed off the top and put it in the best dishes.

That is exactly what happens in industry and business. The cream does rise to the top. Good, enthusiastic workers are promoted. Grumpy, miserable workers are fired, or if they can't be fired, slotted to the dead letter department where they grumble away 80,000 hours of their lives.

Learning to love your job is probably the fastest way to rise above it to another position which is more challenging and interesting and which you can love even more.

Putting your heart and love into the job you now hold does not mean that you are stuck there forever. You can move on when the opportunity arises. In the meantime, you have developed habits of thinking which will serve you wherever you go.

Loving your job isn't like getting married and promising, "Till death do us part." Loving your job is simply a way to propel yourself into an even better one - either here or there. Anywhere you choose.

SKILL BUILDERS

1. Ask yourself what you could do to sharpen your job attitude.
2. Ask yourself what you should do to change your work style.
3. Ask yourself what you hope to be doing one year from now.
4. Make a list of all the things you enjoy about your work.

5. Read your list aloud for a week each morning before work. Notice anything different?

AFFIRMATIONS

...I have wonderful work which pays me well.
...I love my work and I do it well.
...I am loved and appreciated at work.
...My work is fascinating.

TREATMENT

Universal Mind operates in a continuous flow of ideas and creative experiences. I am in the flow of life and my work is an important part of the way I experience the flow of life.

My work is wonderful work and I do it easily and well. I am well paid and very well appreciated for my work. I allow myself to enjoy each moment of my work day and when I finish, I am refreshed and happy. It is a joy to do a job well and I am a joyous person.

I love my work. My work suits me and I attract more and more excellent opportunities to enjoy life through my work. I am a happy worker with an outstanding record of achievement and an excellent attitude.

My work brings me recognition and excellent financial rewards. These rewards are immediate and abundant. There is no delay.

I release this treatment, knowing that right work is mine and that everything associated with work is a positive experience and so it is.

LESSON THIRTY-SIX

MY WORK IS COMPLETED

Some people feel as though they are always behind in their work. Often, people take on more tasks than they can possibly complete and they need to rearrange their schedules. However, a clear mind and a focused attention can work wonders.

You can increase your efficiency greatly through treatment work. Chores go faster and the work goes well when it is backed by affirmations and prayer.

SKILL BUILDERS

1. Take a look at your unfinished work list. Cross out the tasks which are not really necessary.
2. Set priorities by putting stars by the most important tasks.
3. Circle the tasks which have immediate deadlines.
4. Make a plan which allots some time for important tasks which are not urgent.
5. Arrange that plan so the most complicated tasks are tackled early, when you are freshest.
6. Use these simple steps to increase your efficiency.

AFFIRMATIONS

...I get a lot done easily.

...My work goes well.

...I have plenty of time.

...I love my work.

TREATMENT

This day, I turn the job of catch-up over to Universal Mind. I take whatever steps I need to complete all unfinished tasks.

I accept - In Mind - completely catching up on tasks very quickly and easily. I see myself with a clean desk and time to think. I see all bills paid. I see all letters written and mailed. I see all reports in. I see all phone calls made. I see order and peace in my work life.

I accept this as my completed goal and I release any anxiety or fear associated with any of these tasks. Each day I make the decisions I need to make, I take the steps I need to take in order to complete the work. I set realistic goals and work steadily toward completing them. I know I have the power of Universal Mind behind me on this project and that for God, nothing is impossible.

I accept this vision or a new order in my life and so it is.

LESSON THIRTY-SEVEN

I DEMONSTRATE SUCCESS

You are already a success because you are a unique, individualized expression of God. As you come to realize and accept this fact, your life will take on the shape which you call success on a material level.

Define your goals and visualize them daily. You establish your own vision of success and it will be based on your deepest desires and dreams. You are already wonderful and you are in the process of sharing your magnificence with the world in new and wonderful ways.

SKILL BUILDERS

1. Select a person you believe is truly successful and list the attributes he/she has which you admire.
2. Circle the attributes which you share with that person. For instance, a person who admires honesty is usually honest. Notice how well you match your vision of success already.
3. Ask three friends to give you three words which they believe describes your particular brand of success. Write the words down and study them often. You really are wonderful.
4. Make it a point this week to claim your success. Speak only good about yourself.

AFFIRMATIONS

...I am wonderful!

...I am success in action.

...My success is my natural way.

...I cannot fail. I am a winner.

TREATMENT

Divine Intelligence is at work in my life. I am now ready to let Divine Intelligence clean up all pockets of resistance and shame which have heretofore been hidden from the light. I let my light shine.

Specifically, I am now ready to be completely healthy. I am ready to drop all financial problems and be rich. I am ready to catch up on all chores and be order. I am ready to make new friends and love the old ones in a deeper, more meaningful way. I am ready to demonstrate success in every area of my life.

I am ready to love myself completely. I am ready to step out and live.

I let Divine Intelligence support me financially.

I let Divine Intelligence accomplish my goals.

I let Divine Intelligence make me healthy.

I let Divine Intelligence bring people into my life who love, honor and respect me.

I let Divine Intelligence fill my life with love, health, honor, success, beauty and joy.

I wholeheartedly accept this treatment. I turn my face and my body and my hidden mental and psychological corners toward the light. I let this happen right *now. I feel the light drying up old beliefs which no longer serve and I feel the light shining on the wonderful, beautiful successful me that I am. I love myself. I take care of myself. I allow myself to be the best that I can be. And so it is.*

LESSON THIRTY-EIGHT

I LOVE MY BODY

We need to learn to love our bodies as they are right now. It doesn't matter what shape our body is in, it is serving as a vehicle for life. It doesn't matter whether or not we are experiencing a condition which we call illness, our bodies are the precious vessel of the Life Force.

Learn to honor and praise your body and it will respond by assuming the shape you prefer. Learn to honor and praise your body and it will respond by casting aside the mantle of illness and expressing full health.

Your body is a Temple of the Lord. While it is true that it is a temporary dwelling place for Spirit, it is also true that it is a beautiful dwelling place of life and love. You must never say bad or mean things about your body. You must always praise and support the positive.

Your body will respond to the direction you give it. If you say, "I am fat", long enough, it will gain weight. If you say, "I am limber, flexible and strong," consistently, you will see a greater mobility. Thoughts are creative.

SKILL BUILDERS

1. Think of things which you genuinely like about your body and make a list. Say a few of those things out loud today.
2. Make it a point not to say anything negative about your body for one week. If you slip, quickly correct yourself and replace the negative with a positive.
3. Stand in front of the mirror naked and mentally praise your body. Learn to give it "as is" love.

AFFIRMATIONS

...My body is young, strong and flexible.
...My body is slim, trim and beautiful.
...My body is my home and I am happy in it.
...I love my body.
...I love my beautiful, healthy body.
...I am perfect, whole and complete.

TREATMENT

I know that God is love and I am surrounded by, supported by, and immersed in that love. I am never far from home. Nothing about me is distasteful to God. My body - as it is now - at its present size and in its present shape - is one expression of God and one expression of Love.

I now allow myself to enjoy myself as I am - knowing that I am surrounded by God's love and knowing that I am an expression of that love. I let myself be love personified and I acknowledge my true nature right now. I enjoy the feeling of being comforted, rocked, nurtured in the arms of love. I like being alive and being in love.

At the same time I am loving myself as I am, I am allowing myself to change. I know that at the level of absolute reality, I am perfect, whole and complete and that my body is operating in perfect working order.

I now make a decision to let my body to function optimally. I am willing to express more of who I truly am.

As I express more and more of my true nature, I let go of any negatives and my body demonstrates perfect health.

I let myself be myself. I let my light shine out strong and growing. I allow the joy to well up inside me and bubble out over the edges. I let myself go and in the letting go, I also let myself heal. There is no struggle involved in it. I simply let go and let God. And so it is.

LESSON THIRTY-NINE

MY PERFECT BODY

You can develop a body which more closely approximates your ideal by using scientific mental treatment on a regular basis. If you are interested in gaining or losing weight or adding muscle and reducing flab, you may want to include following sensible diet and exercise as a part of your visionary work.

SKILL BUILDERS

1. Put on some soft music and stretch out comfortably. Allow your mind to follow the shape of your body as it is now. Let the music carry you along. Bless your body and choose to love it as it is.
2. Use your mind's eye to survey your body and decide how you would like to change it. Pretend you are made of a substance such as clay and you can subtract and add at will. Shape a perfect body in your mind and mentally accept it.
3. Imagine your perfect body moving easily and with great flexibility. See yourself dancing or running with joy. Enjoy the feeling of freedom and claim it as your natural birthright.
4. Make a list of the parts and features of your body that you particularly like. Get specific. Say, "I love my liver. I love my lungs."

AFFIRMATIONS

...I love my body.

...My body is young, flexible and vigorous.

...I am jumping for joy.

...I am dancing with life.

TREATMENT

There is a Power for Good in the universe and I am now using it to allow my perfect body to take shape on the material plane. I know that at the level of spirit, I am already whole, perfect and complete. At the level of spirit, I have a fluid, flexible, graceful way of being. I am now allowing that to show on the material plane.

In the past, I may have felt a need to hide my beauty but that is no longer true. I allow my light to shine. I allow my beauty to show, knowing that there is nothing to fear.

I am Spirit. I am surrounded by, immersed in and supported by God. I am at one with God. I am never alone, never afraid, never lonely. I control my food choices easily. I follow my exercise plan comfortably. I am at ease with my body.

I let go of excess weight easily because it no longer serves me. I add muscle where I want. I firm my flesh. I let my body be an expression of my true self. I allow my body to reflect my true nature - ever flexible, ever changing, ever joyful Spirit.

I love my life. I love my body. I love myself. And so it is.

LESSON FORTY

NO CHRONIC CONDITIONS

No matter how long a negative condition has existed, it can be erased quickly and easily. Universal Mind knows nothing of time since all takes place in the present tense at the absolute level of reality.

Even though a person may have held onto a difficult relationship, a painful illness, a financial problem or an overwhelming problem for a long, long time, it is not insurmountable. Divine Intelligence always knows the way and there is no obstacle too great.

All conditions or situations can be dissolved through systematic mental treatment. We live in a spiritual universe - a universe where a Universal Intelligence operates through spiritual laws. Those laws are always operating and never change.

What you can conceive and believe you can achieve. No limits!

SKILL BUILDERS

1. Take a look at one condition or situation in your life which has worried or troubled you for a long time.
2. Visualize how your life would be different if that situation were different.
3. Build a mental picture of your life without that particular condition. Begin to "own" that mental picture a moment at a time.

4. Make a plan to treat daily for the dissolution of that particular issue for one month. Set aside ten minutes before bedtime or decide to do your treatment during your morning shower. Think of it as going on a mental diet or starting a mental exercise plan. Reserve judgement for one month. Just do the treatments.

AFFIRMATIONS

...With God, all things are possible.

...There is no such thing as an insurmountable obstacle.

...I can do, be and have whatever I can mentally accept. I now accept:

_____.

TREATMENT

There is One God, One Mind, One Universal Power. I am connected to this Universal Power and I am also surrounded, supported and immersed in this One God.

I live, move and have my being in the One God. Since nothing is difficult or impossible for God, I know that the vision stated in this treatment is easily achieved. I speak the word and God does the work. I now accept it, allowing it to become reality on the relative plane.

I understand that my life is a result of a series of choices I have made over the past and that beyond that - the choices I have made are a result of beliefs I have held. I now change my beliefs and thereby change my life. I do this quickly, easily, painlessly and permanently.

I give up all fear of failure. I give up all thoughts of ugliness or shame. I give up all belief in genetics or family patterns. I give up all beliefs in psychological damage or mental limitations. I give up known and unknown beliefs and opinions and old programming circling around this issue. I clean my mental house.

I change my mind and see myself as I truly am. Right now, I see the real me. I am not limited in any way. I am what I am and that is wonderful. I am whole, perfect and complete and I express that wholeness in every area of my life.

I enjoy life and I especially enjoy making healthy choices. I love to exercise my God-given right to choose the best for myself. Each time I make a healthy choice I feel good about myself and it adds to my consciousness of success.

I radiate health and vitality. I radiate success and beauty. I radiate power and joy. I radiate a real sense of freedom and my new mental atmosphere draws to me wonderful people and experiences.

Right now, I completely and totally accept this vision for myself. I claim it and I nurture it and I let it come into being without fear or resistance. I let Divine Intelligence guide me in every way as I allow the process of changing mind/changing body to work.

I love life this day. And so it is.

LESSON FORTY-ONE

HIGHEST AND BEST

Many of us learned to aim low when we were youngsters. The theory was that we would avoid disappointment if we didn't ask for too much. Of course, that doesn't work nearly as well as asking for a lot and taking the steps which are necessary to achieve the best.

You can have whatever you can imagine for yourself and then actually believe you can have. You are working with spiritual laws which never fail and you are always working to climb higher in your expression of life. You have a right to excel.

SKILL BUILDERS

1. Look back on your youth and write a paragraph about some dream which you let yourself be persuaded was out of your reach.
2. Ask yourself what your dream aimed to deliver. Was it a sense of adventure? Success? Love?
3. Decide what you can do now to achieve your initial goal. You may not be able to start a career as a medical student at 75 but you may find a way to achieve that sense of worthwhile service which your dream was intended to give you.
4. Consider taking steps based on old dreams which have been remodeled.

AFFIRMATIONS

...I deserve the best.

...My dreams do come true.

...I have a highest and best mentality operating in my life.

...I choose to fulfill my promise to myself.

TREATMENT

One God, One Mind, One Power. I am a conduit of power and I speak my word with ease and complete confidence.

I speak the word for highest and best life possible. This life includes fulfilled dreams and promises. It includes right choices, love and peace, a perfect body and wonderful health and great sense of self-worth. It includes right work, wisdom and love and a sense of purpose and accomplishment.

I am fulfilled. I am at peace. I am love. I am truth. I am wisdom and I am forever young.

I know that this treatment is extremely effective because I do not have any resistance at all to its coming into being. This word goes directly into action. And so it is.

LESSON FORTY-TWO

I MOVE FORWARD

Sometimes it takes a while to see any progress in our mental work. We know that spiritual laws are operating and we have a clear vision. As far as we are aware, we are ready to accept success and yet the challenge continues to exist.

It is important to keep on using affirmations and spiritual mind treatments when you hit a snag of this sort. One way to keep going is to imagine that you are chipping away at the problem every time you do a treatment. See the challenge as a log jam and know that this day the whole thing will dislodge and truth will rush in. Do not be discouraged. Know that the work is being done in Mind and that every treatment you give changes something in your consciousness. Know that you will eventually see success and that you already are success.

SKILL BUILDERS

1. Use your imagination to write several different affirmations to approach the same challenge from several different angles. If you are not having any problems at the moment, choose a long term goal such as prosperity and work with that. Try at least 12 different wordings.

AFFIRMATIONS

...*I am never stuck. I am always dancing in the light.*
...*Life is fluid, changeable and fun.*

...I am in the dance of life.

...I am never too early or too late. It is always the right time.

...Time is my friend.

...Dedication pays off handsomely and I am dedicated to success.

TREATMENT

I know that there is a Divine Creative Process working in my life right now. I am in co-partnership with this Divine Creative Process and that my part is directive as well as intuitive. I am aware that more is going on that I can see, feel, hold or touch and therefore, I trust my Divine Partner to support, supply and guide as I move forward in my directive process.

I have a plan and I continue with that plan despite any apparent difficulties or delays. That plan is in effect because I know I am divinely guided. I know that my vision benefits me and others. I accept my vision now.

I trust the process and I trust the Universe to support this planned, divinely guided activity. I am open to guidance and change. I am willing to do whatever is necessary to establish my vision. I trust the Universe to guide me in making choices which support my plan.

I am ready to do whatever else I can to speed up the process of acceptance. I trust the Universe to guide me in making choices which are helpful and supportive and which do not trigger old distress signals. I am willing for the time to be now. And so it is.

LESSON FORTY-THREE

BE HAPPY NOW

Our ultimate aim is recognition of our Oneness with God. Our intermediate aims include health, wealth, love, and creative expression. We plan to be happy when we have achieved all of these aims. However, the great paradox is that the only time in which we will ever be able to be happy is right now.

Do not lose sight of this simple truth. In order to be happy, you must be happy now. You can never be happy in the past or the future. It must be here and now.

SKILL BUILDERS

1. Draw a picture of yourself with a smile on your face.
2. Practice smiling in the mirror several times a day.
3. Use your smile wherever you go. Don't wait till someone smiles at you -smile first!
4. Do something that makes you laugh out loud at least once a day this week. It may be watching old movies or reading joke books or simply watching your dog play but laugh aloud.
5. Make it a point to prepare yourself for your workday by creating a sense of happpiness before you leave the house this week.

AFFIRMATIONS

...I am naturally happy person.

...I am happy right now.

...My middle name is Sunshine.

...I love to smile at strangers.

...I smile for the fun of it.

TREATMENT

Right now, before anything else, I am happy. I am happy to be alive. I am happy to be of service. I am happy to love others. I am happy to work hard. I am happy to be rich.

My life is a wonderful journey inward toward a truth that sets me free. Each day, I take a step closer to the goal of total freedom and total acceptance of my life as God's life. I am involved in a wonderful evolutionary process toward recognizing my own Divinity. I am happy to be evolving upward in my understanding of life and I am happy to be alive.

I never delay happiness. I enjoy each day as it comes. I allow myself to laugh and smile at life's events. I know that happiness is primarily a matter of choice and I choose happiness now. And so it is.

LESSON FORTY-FOUR

NO HIDDEN BLOCKS

Studying Science of Mind is a lifelong activity and no matter how well we know the principles there is always something new to learn. Treatment is a tool for getting what we want. It is also a tool for discovering new direction and depths in our life.

We are involved in a never ending process of growth, deepening wisdom and change. There will never be a time when everything is "fixed" and we can hold the world still and enjoy it. Life will always present challenges and we will always have a chance to learn more about ourselves and our relationship to God.

Never believe you have learned it all or that you have "arrived". While it is true that you can learn much and gain marvelous control over your life, it is also true that we are all in process.

SKILL BUILDERS

1. Jot down some things which have changed for you since you started using this book.
2. Jot down some things you expect to change as you go along.
3. Begin to suggest to yourself before you go to sleep at night that you be given new direction and understanding in your dreams. Keep a record of your dreams for a while.

AFFIRMATIONS

...I am a wonderful work in progress.

...My life is everlasting life and it constantly assumes new forms.

...I am never stuck, never finished. There is always more to know.

...Life is exciting and evolutionary!

TREATMENT

I know that I live in a world where Divine Creative Process is continuously operating in my life. My experience forms and reforms as I change my thinking. I know that this is so and I choose to take control of my life at a deeper, more profound level than ever before. I choose to use the wisdom and knowledge I have gained in my Science of Mind studies in very visible ways.

I choose to let my light show. I choose to let my life reform into a picture which everyone can understand as success. I declare right now that I have the strength, wisdom and courage to handle any challenges which arise as I move along the path of life.

I stop resisting change. I choose to stop hiding from my own spiritual growth. I choose to step up and out into a new and greater plane of experience.

I stand in the light - letting the light of the ages instruct me. I stand near the choir - letting the music of the ages inspire me. I stand my ground - speaking truth in strong and powerful way. I speak from the center of my being and I speak with strength.

I allow myself to be myself. I am all right. I am not afraid.

I am full of joy, full of hope, full of anticipation for the next adventure in life. I am always becoming and that is exactly as it should be.

LESSON FORTY-FIVE

I AM NOT DISCOURAGED

When we begin our Science of Mind studies we often have several issues we are working to change or improve in our life. Some of these issues have been around for a quite a while and we may feel stuck.

It is important not to be discouraged when everything doesn't immediately snap into its perfect place. Remember that you probably would not continue to do the work if everything were absolutely perfect in your life.

While it is not necessary to hold onto problems any longer than we have to, it is necessary to understand that we are learning lifelong skills by attacking these issues.

I began my serious study of Science of Mind in order to achieve emotional balance. I was in a difficult relationship and suffered from discouragement, depression and lack of self esteem. When I started attending church and reading books, I thought I would get out of the relationship quickly and move on to be happy.

Because of my own past and a set of conditions, I stayed in the relationship much longer than others would have believed necessary. All that time I was doing treatment work and building a stronger understanding of principle. My situation improved though it did not immediately change.

By the time I had the relationship issue resolved, I had learned quite a bit about Science of Mind. What I learned has served me well in every area of my life. I can honestly say that I was never stuck and should never have been discouraged. It took what it took and in the meantime, I developed mental and spiritual muscles.

SKILL BUILDERS

1. Write a paragraph describing a time when you felt stuck. How did you eventually resolve it? Would Science of Mind have helped?
2. Ask yourself if you feel stuck now. Why?
3. Resolve to treat daily on any issue which feels stuck. Every treatment changes consciousness.

AFFIRMATIONS

...I am always moving up and out. I am never stuck.

...My treatment work is powerful work.

...I am changing my thinking and changing my life.

...I am committed to positive change.

TREATMENT

I know that Divine Intelligence surrounds and supports my life and that all things are possible with God. I also know that I am directly connected to that Infinite Source of wisdom, truth, power and love called God.

Since I am in the flow of Divine Energy and Love, I can never be discouraged or frightened. I am always creating new experiences and events in my life and I am moving forward in my acceptance of more wealth, more health, more happiness and more love.

I have the patience it takes to open up to more good. I do not delay my choices by worry or doubt. I patiently and lovingly remind myself that God and I are One. I patiently push open my acceptance quotient. I firmly and lovingly push out the barriers and obstacles in my belief system. I choose to change and I allow myself to change in a loving manner.

No matter how firmly fixed some situation may seem, I remind myself that Spirit is always creating new forms. I am willing to release the old and let in the new. I am willing to get better. I am willing to have better. I am willing to be better.

I am never discouraged. I know that God does not know time and that all time is now. I know that I allow myself whatever it takes to attain my vision. I remind myself gently to keep working on my acceptance of good and I do not waste my time or talent on false emotions such as fear, doubt or worry.

I am following my plan. I am in the correct position and frame of mind to let change happen. I choose to keep working on my spiritual growth, knowing that change will manifest as I grow in understanding. I choose to grow in understanding right now. I let this be so and so it is.

LESSON FORTY-SIX

FAST ACTION

Timing can be tricky. On the one hand, you don't want to give up if things don't go quickly. On the other hand, you know that each treatment must be done in the present tense and accepted as being complete now.

Most teacher recommend you do daily treatments on a particular issue until you see results manifested. If you think of the issue at other times during the day, simply say a short affirmation and release it.

Make sure you haven't set up a scenario which requires a certain amount of time. Many demonstrations can be very quick. You can have immediate healings in relationships, health, work and other areas of your life.

In the Infinite Mind, all time is simultaneous. As you deepen your understanding of spiritual matters, you will begin to expect quicker and quicker demonstrations. Instead of expecting a cold to go away in seven days, you may find it goes away in three days. Or you may simply never have colds anymore.

SKILL BUILDERS

1. List some demonstrations you have seen which were very fast.
2. Write a description of one healing you experienced or witnessed which was instantaneous.
3. Look within and find areas which you believe will take time to change. Make a list.

4. Select one long-term goal on your list and treat for it right now. Imagine getting it today. Build a sense of immediacy and acceptance. Surprise yourself!

AFFIRMATIONS

...God doesn't need to tell time.
...With God, all things are possible.
...I live in the here and now.
...This moment is my moment. I am with it.

TREATMENT

I recognize that God is all powerful and present everywhere. For God, there is no time and therefore can be no delay.

I am connected to God. I am immersed in, surrounded by, supported by and connected to God. God and I are one and whatever I can accept, God will produce. It is the nature of God to create new experiences, new conditions, new shapes and forms. There is nothing strange or difficult about getting an immediate demonstration. I now accept an immediate positive change in _____. I accept it right now. I let go of any old notions about time and space and let this be so. I dance through life. I am brimming over with energy, enthusiasm and joy.

I release this treatment, knowing I have released old fashioned ideas about struggle, time and discouragement. I know this treatment sets fast action into motion and that my goal is accomplished in record time with health, beauty, joy and ease.

I let this be so and so it is.

LESSON FORTY-SEVEN

I CHOOSE MY EXPERIENCE

Cultural beliefs and conditioning can be very detrimental to your spiritual growth and treatment work unless you take positive steps to separate yourself from the beliefs of the general population.

Some people avoid reading newspapers and attempt to bury their heads in the sand while they create a special world of their own. I do not recommend that, especially if you are attempting to build financial stability or move up in the work world. You need to know what is going on but you don't need to be a part of it.

As your spiritual knowledge and conviction grows, you will send roots deep down into spiritual soil and you cannot be threatened by outside events. Your life has a definite direction and purpose which cannot be found on the front page of the newspaper. Your financial security is based on spiritual principles, not the financial pages or the Dow Jones Report.

"Be of this world but not in it," the master teacher Jesus advised and it was good advice. Begin to practice knowing the truth no matter what you hear on television.

SKILL BUILDERS

1. Read a news magazine such as *Time* and find at least one story you can rewrite with a Science of Mind slant. For instance, if *Time* reports that the schools are using computers to raise math scores for reluctant learners, show how the belief systems of the students have changed.

2. If you are in a Science of Mind class, ask your teacher to spend a few minutes discussing positive current events each week. If you are on your own, search out your own positive news stories. Learn to read the news with a hopeful eye.

3. Look backward and make a list of positive inventions which have developed in your lifetime.

4. Look backward and make a list of positive social change which you see in your lifetime.

5. Look at today's world and see exciting possibilities for change. Imagine a world without _____ and write a paragraph describing what that would be like.

6. Listen to your conversation. Next time you hear yourself being critical of the government, politicians, world events, educators or business people ask yourself if you want to add energy to those problems. See if you can rephrase your conversation more positively without being hypocritical.

AFFIRMATIONS

...I am a positive world force.

...Let peace begin with me.

...The world is a wonderful place.

...This nation is a wonderful nation.

...The world is getting better and better.

...Exciting new beginnings are happening all over the world.

...I am in charge of my life.

...I create my own experience.

TREATMENT

God is all there is and I am connected, surrounded and immersed in God. Therefore, my word has the power of the Universe backing it.

I know that I choose my own experience by thinking the thoughts I think, believing as I believe and by allowing the prevailing belief systems of my society to carry me along.

This day, I choose to take firmer control of my thoughts than I ever have before. This day, I choose my own experience.

I consciously direct my thoughts toward those experiences which I wish to attract into my life. I allow my mind to dwell on love, health, wealth, happiness, peace and creative accomplishments. I do not waste my energy on worry, doubt, fear or wondering what other people think I should think or do. I choose to be the best example of me that I can.

I choose to step up the amount of creative energy I put into my treatments and affirmations. I choose to expand my vision of myself as a spiritual being. I choose to experience the power which is mine by right of Divine Inheritance. I choose to develop my Science of Mind skills at a new level.

I choose my experience and I choose the very best for myself. I deserve to experience the best and I am aware that the power to deliver the best begins with my decision to let it be.

I let this treatment be the beginning of a new stage of control in my life. I let this treatment be a major step in the direction I want to go. I let this treatment be a signal to myself, to others and to God that I am willing to let go of false beliefs about the past, about fear, about envy, about duty, about karma, about heredity or environment, about anything which may seem to be an obstacle in the path of expressing abundantly.

I accept a new level of responsibility. I accept a new level of controlled power. I accept a new level of prosperity. I accept a new level of love. I accept a new level of life. I choose my experience now. And so it is.

LESSON FORTY-EIGHT

UNLIMITED ENERGY

You are using a Creative Energy in your life which is unlimited. You can have as much of that energy as you can accept in your life. You need never run out of steam or be exhausted.

People who get a lot done are people who have found a way to plug into a reservoir of energy which propels them beyond the ordinary. Your Science of Mind studies can do that for you. Once you get used to the idea that any limitations you are experiencing are a result of your beliefs, you can begin to expand your beliefs. Raise your level of expectation about your energy level and let Divine Intelligence rush to fill the space you have created.

SKILL BUILDERS

1. Go within and use your mind's eye to see your body as filled with white light. Imagine that white light moving through you rather than being static.
2. If you feel tired this week, pause and close your eyes for a moment. See the white light travelling through your body and refilling any dark areas of exhaustion. See the truth that sets you free.
3. Draw a picture of yourself. Now open the picture at the top of your head and draw energy rushing through your body. It enters at the top of your head and circles through your body, leaving by your hands and feet. See yourself as a center of circulating energy.

AFFIRMATIONS

...I have unlimited power at my disposal.

...I have unlimited energy to use.

...I am a creative center of light, love and energy.

...I am always full of life.

...I have fun at work. I have fun at play. I have fun everywhere.

...I love life and life loves me.

TREATMENT

There is an Infinite Power operating in my life which enables me to accomplish a great deal in a short time. I am at one with that Power and I let it flow through me, carrying me along the day's tasks with ease and simplicity.

I work efficiently and well. I approach all my tasks with enthusiasm and confidence. I know that there are no obstacles which cannot be overcome by Divine Mind. I rely on Divine Mind to be my partner in every part of my enterprise.

No task is too difficult. No chore is too onerous. No job is too overwhelming. No activity is too tedious.

I am never discouraged. I am never frightened. I am never bored. I am always in love with life. I am always efficient and light hearted. I am always at one with my Source.

My life is full of wonderful activities and I approach my life energetically. My work brings me excellent rewards immediately as well as in the long run. I take pleasure and pride in all of my endeavors.

I am happy while I work because I am one with God. I am tuned into the power and joy of the Universe. I hear the beautiful music of life expressing itself as I involve myself in the day's activities. I am at ease, at peace and energetic. I can whistle while I work because I enjoy every part of my life. My life is God's living enterprise and it is all good.

LESSON FORTY-NINE

EXPECT THE BEST

Training yourself to expect the best is a good way to spend your spare time. You can mentally redirect your thoughts in the supermarket line, while driving a car, or even during the commercials on television.

Your life will benefit immediately and directly from the mental exercise of replacing worry thoughts with optimistic ones. Not only will you feel better when you let the worry go, you will actually begin to see a difference in the conditions of your life. That's because thoughts are powerful messages to the Universe. We are constantly sending spiritual signals.

In Science of Mind, we believe that spiritual laws respond to your thinking - whether positive or negative. Fear and worry act like lightning rods, attracting trouble as surely as expecting the best insures success. Your thoughts are so powerful that you can chart your future simply by looking at your prevailing belief system.

If you have difficulty seeing your own life in that perspective, look at the lives of your friends and neighbors. The man who complains of poverty usually has no money. The woman who mistrusts her husband eventually drives him away.

Even if you are not ready to fully accept the proposition that your thoughts are controlling the events in your life, you will probably acknowledge that optimism pays off in the response it evokes in other people.

People who like people and expect the best from their friends have more friends than those who avoid others out of fear and mistrust.

Salespeople who expect to make the sale consistently do better than the ones who don't. There is a whole motivational seminar industry built on bringing these simple ideas to business.

Children who expect to do well in school consistently make higher grades than those who have low expectations. Despite the recent criticism, teaching self esteem makes sense because studies prove over and over again that children with high self esteem do well in school and later in life.

Genius is certainly built on directing one's thoughts to the interesting problem at hand rather than worrying about it or attempting to conform to past beliefs in order to solve a challenge. If inventors didn't have the self confidence to try new things we'd still be living in caves.

You can begin to take charge of your life by taking charge of your thoughts and monitoring the results. Your journal should be getting full of excellent proofs of the power of treatment. Remember that you want to notice success and let it register at the conscious and subconscious level in order to build a more powerful level of conviction. As your conviction grows, so will your success level. You've heard of a cycle of despair? You are involved in a cycle of successful living!

By now, your thinking patterns should be changing because of your conscious control in daily affairs. For instance, if you are worried about your marriage you will begin to count the good aspects instead of dwelling on the irritating ones. If you are alarmed about your weight, make a note of the times you exercise and choose food wisely. Give yourself a pat on the back to reinforce intelligent behavior.

Next time you catch yourself worrying about the economy, pause and remind yourself that we are the most creative and generous nation in the world. Then remind yourself that tough times don't last but tough people do.

It is impossible to hold two thoughts at a time so thinking of something positive automatically pushes out the negative ones. It may sound simplistic to say you can change your life by changing your thinking but the results can be observed if you consciously embark on such a program.

SKILL BUILDERS

1. Set your wrist watch alarm or find some other way to notice what your thoughts are several times a day.
2. Gently remind yourself to get back on track. Positive thoughts bring positive results.
3. Begin to form definite time slots in the day to use affirmations, treatments or simply think positive thoughts. Begin the lifelong task of building better thought habits.

AFFIRMATIONS

...I am a positive thinker.
...Every day, in every way, I am more and more positive.
...I am on the right track.

TREATMENT

Infinite Mind now enables me to change my mental direction whenever needed. I am a positive thinker, attracting more and more positive experiences into my life. I love my life and I love the way my thoughts act as magnets for good in my life.

I now release any fear that I am too old to change or that I am too deeply ingrained in negative habits to change. I acknowledge that the nature of life is change and that I am a willing participant in the flow of life.

I change my mind easily and quickly. I release all old, out-moded ideas and replace any negative beliefs with wonderful new thoughts. The building blocks of my mind are constructing a new experience and I am delighted that this is so.

I am unlimited potential and my mind is God's mind. No thought of mine is too difficult to release, too ingrained to erase or too stubborn to abolish. I am a new person, filling my head with wonderful new thoughts. I understand the true meaning of the expression **born again**. *I am renewed in mind and so it is.*

LESSON FIFTY

IMMANENCE OF GOD

The most basic and perhaps the most puzzling concept in Science of Mind is the immanence of God. We can expect to gain understanding of this concept of oneness as we practice and study.

Many of us were raised with the image of God as separate being. This being was usually male and sometimes resembled a kindly uncle who sends us gifts on special occasions if we are good little girls and boys. Some of us were introduced to a fiercer image of an angry judge who found us lacking.

Until we rid ourselves of the notion that God is out there and separate from our lives, we will not come into full understanding or power. We must let go of false images at a conscious and subconscious level in order to prosper from Science of Mind.

Begin to know that God is Creative Intelligence, constantly making new forms and constantly changing. Begin to understand that everything is immersed in God and you are immersed in God as well. Begin to know that you are not separate from God at all. You are a unique and individualized expression of God.

You will come to the realization of your power gradually if you pay attention to your ideas about God.

SKILL BUILDERS

1. Imagine yourself in a circle of light. See yourself as a small dot and then let that dot expand and grow until it becomes the whole circle. Now see the circle expanding until everything in your mind is white light. This is a meditation you can repeat on a regular basis. It will help you understand who and what you are.
2. Begin to focus on the outer edges of people and see the way the edges blur. Play with the idea that forms blend into each other.
3. Visit a museum and look at the way painters handle the edges of forms and the way they handle light. Look at some Impressionist paintings and see the way the painters allow colors and forms to soften and bleed into each other. Does this mean anything to you?
4. Practice looking at people while they are talking and listening with one ear while you affirm, "You are the image and likeness of God," silently. Observe how their reaction changes and how you are able to see how beautiful they are. You are also beautiful.

AFFIRMATIONS

...I am the image and likeness of God.

...I am one with God.

...Divine Love fills and surrounds me.

...God is love in action and I am love in action.

TREATMENT

One Mind. One God. One Universal Intelligence. I live, move and have my being in that One Universal Intelligence. I know this as my central identity and each day I move closer and closer to really understanding and enjoying this knowledge.

I am the living expression of God. I am the way in which God knows itself. I am what I am and that is good. I am light. I am love. I am goodness in action. I am all that is, here and now and forever.

I allow this treatment to open my eyes, expand my mind and bring me closer to understanding the great joy of life. I accept a new vision of myself and so it is.

LESSON FIFTY-ONE

GOD AND I ARE ONE

Mystics consistently report an experience of unity which includes a total relationship with God. This is an experience which must be felt rather than intellectualized but you can begin to grasp your oneness with God by using a variety of metaphors to sense the relationship.

SKILL BUILDERS

1. You are more than a grain of sand on the beach. The beach is also completely contained in your grain of sand. See if that makes any kind of sense to you.
2. Some people think of themselves as a drop of water in the ocean but it might be more helpful to think of yourself as a vase in the ocean which contains water and is surrounded by water. The water in and outside the vase is exactly the same water.
3. Some people think of themselves as a wave on the water. They know themselves as God in action. Electricity can be described as a wave and a particle. Can you see yourself as a wave on the surface of water and a particle in the water?
4. Water, ice and steam are all the same but they are in different forms. Can you think of yourself as an ice cube in a glass of water?
5. Think of one snowflake in a snowstorm. Think of one yellow flower in a hillside of blossoms. Think of yourself as a thickened cloud in a sea of air.

6. Decide which of these images it would be easiest for you to use in your studies. None of these images is true but they all begin to hint at the truth. You and God are one. You are not a part of God and you are not all of God. But every part of you is God and all of God is in every part of you. Have fun with this - it will be easier and easier for you to grasp as you practice Science of Mind.
7. Your mind is directing Creative Intelligence to make ever changing forms in your life. Envision the experiences in your life as a series of clouds moving across the sky. What shapes would you change? How would you like health to picture itself? How would you like wealth to picture itself? How would you like love to picture itself? How would you like creativity to picture itself?
8. Put on some great music and close your eyes. Watch the clouds move and shift into shapes you choose. You are a creative genius in action.

AFFIRMATIONS

...I am creative genius in action.

...I am beautiful and wonderful.

...I am surrounded by and immersed in God's love.

TREATMENT

God is all there is and I am surrounded, supported, immersed in and a microcosm of that wholeness, that Divine Unity which we call God.

I now open my mind, my heart and my will to experiencing more of my oneness of God than I have experienced before. I am ready to fully understand the truth. I am ready to fully experience the glorious unity of my true nature.

I know that the Bridegroom rushes to meet the Bride and that as soon as I am truly ready to know the truth, it will be my experience. I resolve to be ready right here and now and so it is.

LESSON FIFTY-TWO

A FINAL WORD ABOUT CHURCH ATTENDANCE

I believe people who attend church on a regular basis experience great benefit in their lives for several reasons.

The most obvious reason for church attendance is that it breaks the pattern of the week and directs us to spiritual matters in a very specific, concrete way. Listening to a sermon, performing rituals, singing songs all serve to remind us that our essential nature is spiritual.

Beyond the conscious recognition of our spiritual natures, regular church attendance stimulates the mind. Your minister is a person who has spent a major portion of her/his life thinking about our relationship to God. Even if we do not agree with everything we hear, the talk will stimulate our own thinking.

Religious Science is a teaching which encourages intellectual questioning and tends to attract thinking people. It is a mental science, not an emotional experience, although we deal with changing beliefs and that means dealing with emotions. In my church, it is normal for people to listen with an alert mind. They often take notes, sometimes writing questions and comments on the order of service and turning their thoughts in with their contribution. I appreciate the feedback, and often find their questions a good platform to begin another Sunday talk.

For example, I was once talking about the joys of expressing love in our lives and I got a question about how to control chronic loneliness. The picture painted by the writer was a desperate one and it served to remind me that there are some in every congregation who simply don't know how to make the first move by reaching out to others. On another Sunday, I spoke about alleviating the condition of loneliness in a very practical manner.

In Religious Science we teach that every person is spiritual at all times and that every day is a spiritual experience. Understanding this does not remove the need for church attendance - it increases it.

The whole point of our wonderful teaching is to arrive at a place where we are constantly aware of our oneness with God. What better place to take steps toward that awareness than with like minded people? It reinforces our weekday efforts.

We do not believe in separating religion from life. Nor do we believe that isolation is a holy condition. We believe that Science of Mind is to be used on a daily basis in our daily lives.

Another good reason to go to church is to meet people who are travelling the same spiritual path you have chosen. Church serves as a very effective support group. It helps to know that no matter how unusual your beliefs seem to be in the work place, there are people you meet on Sunday and in classes who know you are on the right track.

We are involved in learning to look at the world with new eyes instead of through a glass darkly. We are learning to see peace, prosperity and health in our daily lives, despite the news on television or unpleasant work conditions. We will succeed much faster if we seek the support that church offers us.

The other reason to attend on a regular basis is that commitment is good for people. Especially in Southern California which offers a rootless, surface experience to some. Anywhere at all, there is joy in deciding to really belong to a spiritual community. The bonding between others is wonderful but even more important is the self satisfaction that comes from finding a positive program for growth and change and sticking to it.

IF YOU CURRENTLY ATTENDING CHURCH ON A SPORADIC BASIS, I CHALLENGE YOU TO ATTEND EVERY WEEK FOR SIX MONTHS AND SEE THE DIFFERENCE IN YOUR LIFE. YOU WILL BE AMAZED AND PLEASED AT THE RESULTS.

ABOUT THE AUTHOR

Jane Claypool is founder and pastor of the CENTER FOR POSITIVE LIVING, *Carlsbad Religious Science Church* in Carlsbad, California.

She is also the author of *Wise Women don't worry, Wise Women don't sing the blues* which is published by Cornucopia Press.

She is author of 75 books for young adults and children. In 1981, she was awarded Writer Of The Year by the Society For Children's Book Writers. She has published hundreds of feature stories, plays and articles as well as books. Her young adult books have been translated into nine different languages and have sold millions of copies. She writes under the names Veronica Ladd and Jane Claypool Miner as well as Jane Claypool.

Currently, she is serving on the Religious Science International Board of Education as Curriculum Director. She is also President of the San Diego Chapter of the New Thought International Alliance.

A talented facilitator, Claypool leads workshops and seminars all over the nation. She especially enjoys leading weekend retreats. She is a popular speaker at metaphysical events, women's organizations, in corporations and at writer's conventions. She has appeared on local and national television many times.

The ministry is her fourth career and she believes she has been in training for it all of her life. She has been a writer, a teacher, a realtor and a sales and marketing director for a real estate development company.

Claypool can be contacted through the Center For Positive Living or Cornucopia Press.

For more information contact:
Cornucopia Press
P.O. Box 230638
Encinitas, CA 92023
(760) 633-4400
FAX (800) 313-5116